What They
Thriving in Thin Air

MW01506123

"This timely book makes accessible to all the path to resilience charted by the science of psychology."

Florence L. Denmark,
Distinguished Research Professor, Pace University
Past-President American Psychological Association– 1980 - 81

"Thriving In Thin Air is full of practical approaches, accessible models, and step-by-step processes—supported by proven scientific theory. The personal examples from the author's life and the "for instance" work scenarios of today really capture the tumultuous nature of our current climate."

Elliott Masie
Chair, The Learning CONSORTIUM and CEO, The Masie Center

"Flanagan is a bright light during these dark times. This book provides a practical path forward to reversing the rising tide of anxiety that is disabling our workforce. It is pragmatic and inspirational."

Doron Grosman
President/CEO GCT Global Container Terminals

"Great change creates great opportunity for innovation. It can also be highly stressful. In Flanagan's timely and much-needed book he has cracked the code on how to survive person- ally – and thrive professionally – as an innovation pioneer in business and government."

Bryan Mattimore
Chief Idea Guy, Growth Engine Innovation Agency
Author, *21 Days to a Big Idea* and *Idea Stormers*

Dr. Flanagan's book helps to manage our new reality of daily overload and shows us a path to a successful and happy life. A must read for every stressed-out person needing a way to regain order, direction and regain happiness in their lives.

James Dunleavy
Director Rehabilitation Services, Trinitas Regional Medical Center
Mayor, Teaneck, New Jersey

"Leo translates neuroscience into a "how to" manual for today's leaders and the next gen- erations of leaders to be emotionally, cognitively, and socially prepared for the challenges of today and the opportunities of tomorrow."

George Bradt
Chairman of the Board, PrimeGenesis

THRIVING IN
THIN
AIR

Developing Resilience in Challenging Times

Leo F. Flanagan, Jr., PhD

Thriving in Thin Air
Developing Resilience in Challenging Times

ISBN: 978-1-7367591-0-3

Published by
The Center for Resilience, LLC

Cover Design by Eric Labacz

To My Wife Maureen Ellen Flanagan
You Made All The Good Things In Our Life Possible

CONTENTS

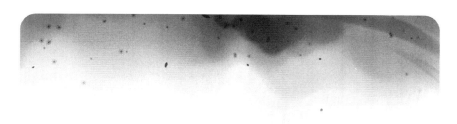

CHAPTER 1

LIVING IN A WORLD
OF THIN AIR

*If you are highly stressed or overwhelmed and want to imme-
diately get started feeling better, go to Chapter 4: Pragmatic
Optimism: The First Factor to Concentrate On. Begin developing that resilience factor. After five days, go to Chapter 5:
Focus—the second master resilience factor. Add that to what
you are doing to build your Pragmatic Optimism. After five
days go to Chapter 6: Building Empathy. Add that and practice what you learned in all three chapters for two weeks. Then
return here and start reading the rest of this book.*

It's not a metaphor anymore. When I first sat down to write this
book, I decided the title *Thriving in Thin Air* was a metaphor for our
emotions, thoughts, and relationships being choked by the digital
deluge. Like all of us I had no idea that the deadly coronavirus disease 2019 (COVID-19) would literally cause (as of this writing) more
than 2.2 million deaths because people could no longer breath. More
than 100 million more people have been infected, battling the virus's
attempt to cut off oxygen. Recently several new variants of the virus
have been identified. One variant – coming from the B.1.1.7 lineage
of the virus – is 50 – 70% more infectious. The U.S. President's Chief
Medical Advisor, Dr. Anthony Fauci confirmed that the B.1.1.7 variant
is not only more infectious it is more deadly[1]. More infectious strains

of the virus will cause the current wave to continue. The U.S. reached 400,000 COViD deaths on January 19, 2021. It is predicted to reach 500,000 deaths by February 4, 2021.

Nor did I anticipate that on May 25, 2020, George Floyd would be murdered while crying out "I can't breathe" as his killer used his knee to choke him for eight minutes and 46 seconds—a murder that may only have come to the world's attention because of iPhone cameras and social media.

Mr. Floyd's murder by a Minneapolis police officer sparked protests across the United States and around the world. The protests placed untold numbers of peaceful protestors at risk of infection with COVID-19 and the possibility of losing their own ability to breathe. It also placed them at risk of being assaulted by police and the National Guard. Perhaps the most infamous assault on peaceful protesters began at 6:17 p.m. on Monday, June 1, 2020. It was at that moment the police and officers from other agencies began advancing on peaceful protesters in Lafayette Square in front of the White House. Batons, shields, flash bang grenades, mounted officers, and chemical agents were used against the protesters. According to *The New York Times*[i], protesters were pursued into the night sometimes with military helicopters flying low enough to scatter people with the downdraft from their propellers.

On January 6, 2021 both houses of the U.S. Congress met to perform the mostly ceremonial counting of the Electoral College votes and certify that Joseph R. Biden was the fairly and legally elected next President of the United States. Since November's election day Donald Trump and his surrogates had relentlessly been spreading what is now known as the "big lie". Telling the U.S. public, indeed the world, that the presidential election had been stolen from him.

Mid-day the President and his surrogates incited an angry crowd of supporters to storm the Capitol Building. They sacked the Capital while attempting to hunt down the Vice President of the United States as well as other prominent leaders. Horrifically, Thriving In Thin Air became relevant to the members of Congress who donned gas masks to protect themselves from tear gas disbursed by both rioters and police. The assault was an act of domestic terrorism perpetrated by anarchists, fascists, and racists. An act that will hopefully spur on a focus on eliminating systemic racism.

Systemic racism is not unique to the U.S. As journalistic Justin Worland reported "Around the world, racial and ethnic minorities have demanded justice after centuries of structural discrimination."[2]

The members of Congress did thrive as they returned to their chamber that very night to finish the task interrupted by violence, threats to their lives, and the deaths of five individuals.

The economic and social shutdowns across the globe have dramatically increased the numbers of homeless and hungry. Racial and ethnic minorities around the globe have been disproportionately harmed by COVID-19, systemic racism, and all the aspects of historic unemployment and poverty.

COVID-19 is the source of a deadly pandemic that has resulted in the systemic problems we humans face around the world coming into sharp relief. Systemic problems include disparities in education; systemic racism; the fragility of global supply chains; endemic poverty and the

Figure 1: Systemic Problems in Focus 1

millions upon millions who are only days or weeks from falling into it; hunger and food security; homelessness and uninhabitable housing; and global warming. In the United States all of these problems are exacerbated by the extremely divisive relationship between the two political parties and the lack of a strategy for dealing with COVID-19, the economic disruption (particularly as it threatens small businesses), and the opportunity to seize the moment to reduce systemic racism.

Before COVID-19's spread across the globe, the World Health Organization called stress the "health epidemic of the 21st century." [1] As a result of the combination of these crises we are in the midst of a growing global mental health crisis. According to the UN,[iii] "The mental health and wellbeing of whole societies have been severely impacted by this crisis and are a priority to be addressed urgently."

The signatures of this growing global mental health crisis are anxiety and depression. Anxiety and depression are experienced because we are surrounded by existential threats with no clarity as to how or when they will end and a lack of personal choices (i.e., control) in how we can respond to them.

Of the crises we face, the anxiety/depression pandemic is in many ways the most threatening. Anxiety will interfere with our ability to reliably follow safety precautions until the COVID-19 vaccines are in widespread use. Anxiety will interfere with our ability to participate in the reopening of our societies and economies. Anxiety will be a barrier to dialogue, agreement, and adoption of social justice reforms and solutions to educational, economic, and health disparities.

Anxiety is also compounded by the grief that has taken hold of us in reaction to all the crises we are facing. We are grieving multiple losses all at once.

First, there is the usual grieving. The loss of loved ones through natural causes and accidents. The loss through divorces. The grief we feel when we or someone we know is diagnosed with a terminal illness. All these sources of grief are part of the natural fabric of our lives.

We then are grieving the millions of people who have been infected—many of whom, while recovered, face lifelong deleterious effects of having the disease. Of course, we grieve those who died of the virus.

Then there are dozens of losses in our daily freedoms we grieve: the inability to stop into our favorite coffee shop without donning a mask or having "take out only"; the inability to go to the local library or a movie or concert; and no longer being able to hug friends and family. These types of losses mount up, adding to our grieving.

The shutdown of our economy creates yet more sources of grief. Families that own small businesses—some for generations—grieve over bankruptcy wiping out their livelihoods and ways of life. Students who are no longer able to find part-time and summer jobs are now having to postpone their education. Families are forced to move because they can no longer afford the rent.

Racism ignites many sources of grief including the families, friends, neighbors, and communities of George Floyd and all African Americans who have lost their lives at the hands of police. African American parents grieve that in 2020 they still must give their sons "the talk" about how to interact with police officers when stopped without cause. This grief is shared by people of various racial and ethnic groups around the world.

In the U.S. and many other nations, the white majority grieves over the realization that we have permitted racism in its most lethal and ugly forms to continue by turning a blind eye. In other nations those who perpetrate racism are not white.

Healthcare providers are grief-stricken in having to hold iPhones next to the ears of dying patients so they can hear tearful goodbyes from their loved ones as they pass away. As the first wave of the virus surges once again, physicians are now beginning to decide who will be put on a ventilator and who will not. A true life and death decision. Grief consists of five components: bargaining, anger, denial, sadness, and acceptance. We do not progress through these stages in any kind of predictable or orderly fashion—even when we are only grieving one loss. In the maelstrom of grieving that we are living through, we bounce from one source of grief to another, simultaneously changing the emotional component we feel. The storm of grief exponentially increases our anxiety.

With this backdrop why read this book? Why write this book?

Because the latest neuroscience proves that we can build our resilience to first control and then reduce our anxiety to healthy levels, allowing us to navigate ourselves, our families, our communities, and our businesses forward.

This is not a book about hope; it is a book that provides you with the certainty of being able to build your resilience and the resilience of those around you, as well as your businesses, schools, and communities.

Our definition of resilience is precise: the ability to thrive amid adversity. Resilience is not about surviving or using some rebranded short-term coping and stress management techniques. Resilience is about literally rewiring your brain to thrive; it's the ability to build new patterns of behaving, thinking, and feeling that prevent you from being debilitated by stress in the first place.

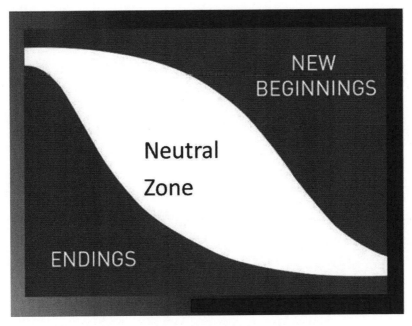

Figure 2: he Bridges Model of Transformation
Adapted from William Bridges Associates

I want you to focus on this good news. It is possible not to be burned out in this present world we live in and to thrive while we succeed and move forward to a new, healthier, and more just world.

We are living in the most stressful threatening environment of our lives. Yet this is also the time when we have the greatest chance of making real systemic change. Here's why. The diagram above is adapted from the work of William Bridges. In his original model, he called the white zone of "uncertainty" the "neutral zone." Neutral doesn't resonate as a description of where humanity sits today. My colleague Roger Sherman has related to me that the zone of uncertainty is to the Buddhists "the land of no longer and not yet." While I haven't found a source for this quote, it certainly resonates with where we are. A phrase not of Neutrality (as in Bridges' original model) but of tremendous uncertainty. We have left much if not most, of life as we knew it behind. While the media, pundits, government leaders, and just ordinary people talk of "returning" and "reopening," this is simply not what we will experience. What we will experience is moving forward into a world of new beginnings. Let's talk about these three phases of our past, current, and future collective experience.

Endings

Dave Coplin, Chief Envisioning Officer at Microsoft UK, coined the term "digital deluge" in his book[iv] to describe the overwhelming amount of input we are bombarded by each day from all technologies. During Endings (where we were pre-COViD) the bombardment had literally reached the point of exceeding our brain's ability to perceive, much less process, incoming information (see Figure 3).

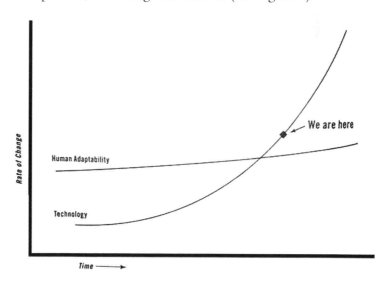

Figure 3: The Rate of Change in the Human
Brain's Capacity vs.Technology Inputs

To me, that meant we were running out of the air (meaning emotional, cognitive, and social space) needed to live life. The thousands of distractions we experienced each day depleted the air we need in which to think. The emotional air surrounding us was becoming increasingly toxic. Social relationships and our sense of community were becoming empty voids similar to the deepest reaches of space. Digital "connections" were replacing the warmth of human contact and physical presence.

Almost 50 percent[v] of the US workforce reported they were emotionally exhausted, cynical, and didn't feel like what they do makes a difference.[vi] In other words, they were burned out.

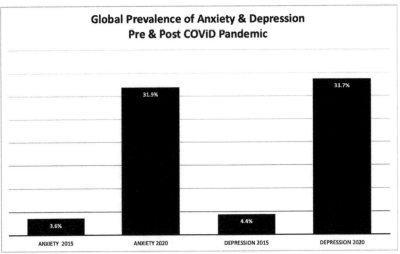

Source 2015 data: Depression and Other Common Mental Disorders: Global Health Estimates. Geneva: World Health Organization; 2017
Source 2020 data: Salari, Nader, et al.. Prevalence of stress, anxiety, depression among general population during COViD-19 Pandemic: A systematic review and meta-analysis. Global Health; 16(1):57 2020 07 06

Figure 4: Global Presence of Anxiety & Depression
Pre and Post COViD Pandemic

On our college campuses 51 percent of undergraduates showed signs of major depression. Being burned out is not a sign of personal dysfunction or failure. Burnout is produced by the world we live in—the air we breathe. I'll talk more about the toxic air that is surrounding us later.

To be certain, burnout and the mental health crisis are not uniquely American. They are global. The most recent global mental health data shows the meteoric rise of both these disorders. In 2015, 3.6% of the world's population met the criteria for an anxiety disorder.[3] In July of 2020, that skyrocketed to 31.9% of the globe's population.[4] In 2015, 4.4% of the world's people met the criteria for a depressive disorder. By July of 2020 that had risen to 33.7%. The vast majority of these spikes occurred in and because of the phase of tremendous uncertainty experienced during the pandemic.

The global state of mental health in the "Endings" phase we left behind was already spiraling out of control. The same is true for all of the other crises that are in stark review. Global warming continued to bring the world toward the brink of environmental catastrophe. Racial injustice against African Americans in the United States and to various peoples around the globe seemed to grow ever more deadly.

COVID-19 is called a "novel" virus, but the fragility and disparity in healthcare systems around the world existed long before they were tested by the deadly disease.

This is not to say that progress wasn't made in our Endings phase. In his book *Factfulness*,[ix] the late Hans Rosling and his colleagues identified 10 biases that lead us to see the world as more bleak than it really is. For example, while poverty is still a tremendous problem, the number of people around the globe living in extreme poverty has been cut in half over the past two decades. Despite super storms and other tremendous natural disasters, the truth is that the number of people killed each year by natural disasters has also be halved over the last 100 years. We've also made great strides with disease prevention in that 80 percent of the globe's one-year-olds have been vaccinated against at least one disease.

Even when analyzing the facts that prove such progress on so many fronts around the globe, Rosling cautioned that we face the likelihood of some terrifying crises. Based on his analysis, the five global risks we should worry about are:

- A global pandemic
- Financial collapse
- Extreme poverty
- Climate change
- World War III

The book was published in 2018, two years before the world has been gripped by the first four of these five risks. The pandemic has resulted in financial collapse and extreme poverty around the world.

Uncertainty

Uncertainty is the phase we are in right now. In my opinion, we will be in the Uncertainty phase for at least a few years—a few years of what may be a once in a millennium opportunity to create and move forward into a systemically better world. Here's why.

Bridges and his colleagues developed this model to understand transformation in organizations such as businesses, nonprofits, governments, and communities. In those cases, Uncertainty was limited to one organization or perhaps an industry. Most of the rest of the world was still back in the Endings phase or the "old days," which allowed people to resist going through Uncertainty and into New Beginnings by clinging to the things that hadn't changed.

For example, in 1992 I was invited to the headquarters of Eastman Kodak in Rochester, New York, to attend a meeting of the company's high-potential talent—the 35 people that Kodak believed would be the best future senior leaders of the iconic company. The purpose was to introduce Kodak's new leadership competency model (i.e., the prescribed recipe for success going forward). Then Chairman/CEO Kay Whitmore spoke for about an hour during which he described the radical changes that Kodak must go through to return to its glory days. Furthermore, each attendee was given a large, red and gold binder of several hundred pages describing the new leadership competency model in great detail.

A 15-minute break was called. While getting a cup of coffee at the back of the room, I overheard three of the participants discussing Whitmore's comments. Their reactions were captured by one quote in particular: "When I was invited to headquarters, I was concerned we were in for some radical change. I'm really glad that nothing significant is going to be different." That's how powerful human denial can be toward the need for change. Today Eastman Kodak is a shadow of itself, not having been able to mobilize its leadership and people to transform quickly enough.

At Kodak, as in so many other iconic companies, people resist change by hanging on to the Endings. Since 1521 when Spanish conqueror Hernan Cortez literally burned his ships so his men had no choice but to follow him to conquer the Aztec people, leaders have known if there is any hope of returning to the past, people will cling to it. Today we refer to that as the need for a "burning platform." The "heat" of staying where you are has to be so intense that you have no other choice but to leave where you are.

In today's world everything is in the Uncertainty phase at once. Globally, people are becoming infected with the virus with too many perishing from it. Total societies and economies have shut down to stem

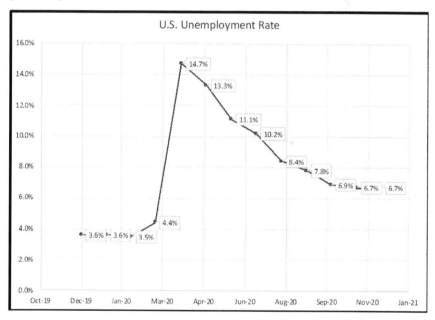

Figure 5: US Unemployment Rates From August 2018 to December 2020. Source: U.S. Bureau of Labor Statistics.

the spread of the disease. As a result, we live with little or no clarity about the way forward. We don't face clear choices about what to do. Every aspect of our lives—from how and when to ride public transportation to shopping for food to communicating with colleagues and loved ones—has changed.

As I write this, across the United States businesses and communities are reopening in some geographies while entire nations and states are shutting down for the second time e.g., the United Kingdom and the State of California. People are outright refusing to wear masks. People are congregating by the thousands at political rallies, by the thousands at beaches, and by the hundreds at bars and restaurants with little or no adherence to safety measures.

Against this backdrop, 25 million people have been infected with COVID-19 in the United States. The number of hospitalizations has spiked overwhelming the capacity of the healthcare system.

The US unemployment rate spiked to over 14 percent in March 2020; as of December 2020, it is still at 6.7 percent. The fear is that the current surge will drive back the progress made on the employment front.

Despite months of peaceful protests since the murder of George Floyd, Congress has yet to pass any police reforms as more African American men are killed.

In short, there is little, if anything, of the past to hang on to. That is the silver lining in this horrible situation. With unprecedented levels of uncertainty, the ability to deny the need to change and move forward is at a historic, global low.

Public relations firm Weber Shandwick and its consultancy United Minds is sending the right message and giving the best guidance to its clients. The message is: We must go forward into the New Beginnings. We should not and we cannot focus on or wish for the ability to return to or reopen the Endings phase. The path of great promise is to move forward, systemically addressing the most significant problems that plague our world.

To capture that promise we must be able to reduce the anxiety and other forms of emotional distress that have become rampant. With certainty we can do that by building our resilience. We can thrive amid adversity as we go forward.

New Beginnings

As we live in the phase of Uncertainty, neither you nor I can foretell what the next phase of our journey will be like in any detail. What we can predict is that if we build our ability to thrive amidst adversity and commit to solving humanity's most systemic challenges, we can go forward to a truly better, more equitable, healthier world. Now is the time.

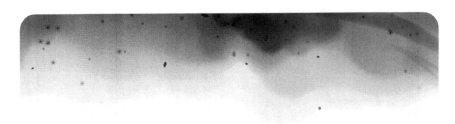

CHAPTER 2

THE NEUROSCIENCE
OF RESILIENCE

Scientists used to believe that the human brain was a pretty fixed structure. Specifically, it was thought that you had a fixed number of brain cells. If any were damaged, new brain cells (neurons) could not be grown. It was also believed that the connections between brain cells (neuro networks) grew to a certain age or point and then the network was fixed.

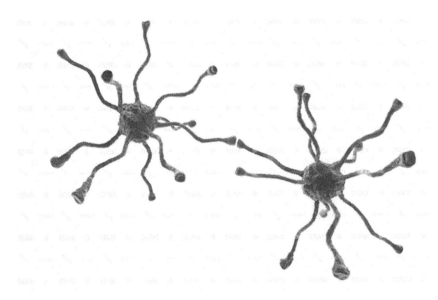

Figure 6: Two Brain Cells Forming a New Connection

The good news is the scientists were wrong. Neuroscientists armed with new technologies to study brains (e.g., MRIs) have proven that the human brain is an incredibly powerful and adaptive organ.

The human brain on average has 100 billion neurons. Each neuron is capable of connecting to networks consisting of tens of thousands of other neurons. A healthy brain is constantly building and paring (deleting) neural networks. The picture below shows two neurons when they are stimulated to form a new connection, or synapse, between them. The neuron on the right is extending its axon to come close to the other neuron's dendrite, leaving a small gap between them. Neurons communicate with each other by sending chemical neurotransmitters or electric charges across these gaps.

As you read this book, thousands of neurons are seeking to connect to each other. Connections are called synapses, which are tiny gaps between neurons. Building new neural networks is how we create new memories, learn, and perform new behaviors.

If you consistently use a new neural network over a period of about 60 to 70 days, the network is protected with a substance called myelin. Figure 7 depicts how myelin—which looks like a string of ziti pasta—has covered the neuron's axon to protect it.

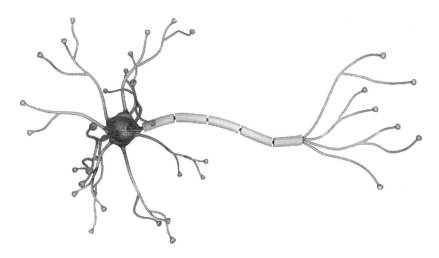

Figure 7: Brain Cell With Myelin Protecting Its Axon

At the same time the brain is insulating neurons and networks that are consistently used, it is paring or eliminating neurons and networks that are rarely used.

In many cases the brain generates new neurons through a process called neurogenesis.

Through these processes of creating new and deleting old connections and generating new neurons, the brain is constantly changing. This process of constant change is called plasticity. As Professor Michael Merzenich,[5] one of the world's leading neuroscientists, puts it: "Your brain—every brain—is a work in progress. It is 'plastic.' From the day we're born to the day we die, it continuously revises and remodels, improving or slowly declining, as a function of how we use it."

New experiences, emotions, and behaviors all trigger the brain to change or rewire itself. The key thing to remember is that your brain and my brain are constantly rewiring based on whatever new experiences we are exposed to on a consistent basis.

As I write this, people around the world have been living in a high state of anxiety and fear for well over 70 days. That means that their brains have often been rewired to stay anxious and to stay at a high level of alert. This is what is causing the global crisis in mental and emotional health.

We have the opportunity—and we know how—to rewire the brain to reduce anxiety and enable us to thrive amid the adversity and uncertainty we are surrounded by. If we practice resilience-building behaviors consistently over a period of 60 to 70 days, we will rewire the brain to think, feel, and act resiliently while eliminating neural circuits that negatively impact our emotional and physical health and behavior. The behaviors are described in Chapter 3: Resilience: The Science of Thriving Amidst Adversity.

Now let's talk about the parts of the brain that we want to rewire.

One of the earliest parts of the human brain to develop is the amygdala. It is the central part of the limbic system. The limbic system creates emotional responses as well as plays a role in creating memories (see Figure 8).

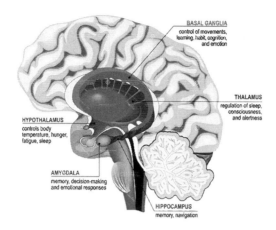

Figure 8: The Limbic System 1

While we refer to the amygdala in the singular, there are actually two amygdala—one on each side of the brain. Its primary job is to help us avoid threats to our survival. Way back in time those threats were often life-threatening. Today most of us don't face life-threatening dangers every day. Clear exceptions include military people in war or conflict zones and those who live or work in the wilderness. In Figure 8, you can see that the amygdala is positioned at the very base of the skull right around the spinal cord. Its influence radiates out and above.

When you perceive a threat, the amygdala activates the flight-or-fight response. The amygdala begins activating the fight-or-flight response by flooding our system with adrenaline, cortisol, and other stress hormones. We feel the results of this flooding immediately. Our heart pumps faster, our breathing becomes more rapid, our palms sweat, and we can start to tremble in our arms, legs, chest, and voice. Our face literally may turn red.

The amygdala shuts off the pathway to our prefrontal cortex—the thinking, rational part of the brain. We're no longer able to analyze the situation and make decisions. We're unable to see anyone's point of view. We are driven to find a path to safety. Daniel Goleman coined the term "amygdala hijack" to describe this experience. The amygdala has literally taken over our reaction to the threat.

Our memory is also compromised. We can't recall facts or experiences that might help us address the threat calmly and productively. All we can attend to is the intense and flashing danger signal the amygdala is sending out to prepare to take one of two actions: fight or flight. We're on autopilot.

Let's look at how this works in today's world. You're watching a cable talk show. You see a confusing stream of images from Dr. Fauci and other health experts warning about the danger that the pandemic may spiral out of control. You see chart after chart showing COVID-19 spiking in various states. You see people out and about across the country as it reopens—people who aren't taking precautions, and on and on. This toxic stew is frightening, triggering the amygdala to activate the fight-or-flight response. Immediately, you have lost the ability to carefully consider and make decisions based on the information that has been flooding you.

Your entire body is mobilized to act. Yet you can't. In the moment you can't physically fight a pandemic or economic disruption or racism. You also can't take flight to safety. So the amygdala continues to sense danger and keeps flooding your system with stress hormone.

Here's what looks like compared to the prolonged stress response:

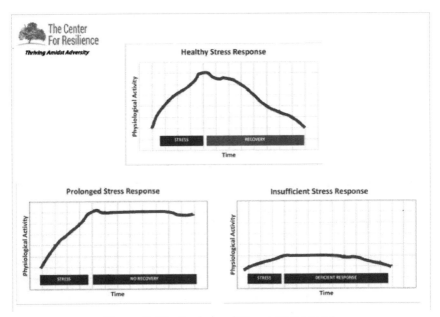

Figure 9: The Prolonged Stress Response 1

The threat is perceived, the amygdala triggers the response, and your level of activation quickly rises. The problem is since you can't eliminate the threat through fight or flight—and you lack the cognitive capability to see other options—your level of activation stays high. Your anxiety becomes overwhelming.

Eventually, your brain and the rest of your body can no longer maintain such a high level of activation. So your level of physiological activity collapses, as you can see in Figure 10.

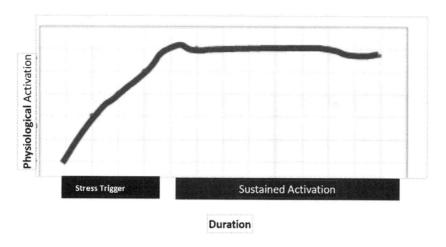

Figure 10: The Inadequate Stress Response

You are mentally, emotionally, and physiologically exhausted. You may begin to feel depressed or develop any number of unhealthy physiological, emotional, or behavioral patterns. In the current environment and many other crisis situations, people rally and accomplish amazing things. On a daily basis I speak to CEOs and Chief Human Resources Officers who insist "Our people are doing fine. They are really amazing." Agreed. They are really amazing, often heroic. But heroism is neither a strategy nor is it sustainable. The problem is eventually they will collapse with exhaustion. In typical disasters in which the initial crisis is time-bound, first responders and ordinary people respond heroically to help and save others. It's not until they return from responding to the immediate crisis response that they crash physiologically, cognitively, and emotionally. In a world of multiple sustained crises, people will perform at heroic levels made possible by the rush of adrenaline and cortisol until the point of emotional collapse.

That is why it's critical that we invest in the development of resilience for ourselves and our loved ones, and those we work with. Resilience can enable us to have a healthy response to stress so we are activated and then recover (see figure 11).

Importantly, we can also rewire our brains so that the amygdala no longer hijacks us. We can maintain the ability to use our prefrontal cortex to make rational assessments, see options, and take healthy and effective actions to move forward. The science tells us how to do this.

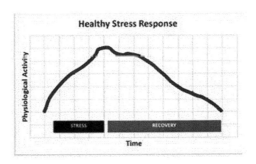

Figure 11: The Healthy Stress Response

Now let's take a quick look at the prefrontal cortex, what it does, and what we want to rewire it to do.

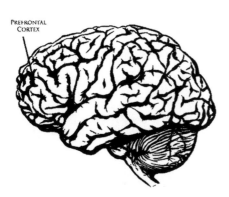

Figure 12: The Healthy Prefrontal Cortex

The prefrontal cortex (PFC) sits right behind your forehead. It carries out the executive functions, which include self-control, analysis, planning, developing options, decision-making, and problem-solving. The PFC allows us to decide what actions to take and then communicates to other parts of the brain and the body to take them. It regulates emotions, thoughts, and actions. Research has shown that we can increase the strength of the PFC as part of building our resilience. When we do that the PFC can counterbalance the amygdala, blocking its ability to "hijack" us. The PFC can allow us to see other perspectives and options for responding to what the amygdala views as a threat. In turn, this gives us the ability to maintain a healthy stress response and take actions that keep our response to threats or conflicts from spiraling out of control.

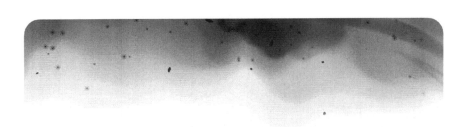

CHAPTER 3

RESILIENCE: THE SCIENCE OF THRIVING AMIDST ADVERSITY

B ased on a meta-analysis of the existing—and rapidly growing—body of research on how to be resilient, I've organized a model of 10 factors that you can develop to become resilient so that the life you live in today's world is fulfilling and rewarding. People who develop their resilience gain a wide range of benefits (see Figure 13).

Some Benefits Of Building Your Resilience

17% More Productive	26% Better Decision-Making
60% Fewer Errors	25% More Proactive
32% Increase In Physical Well-Being	29% Increase In Positive Emotions
25% Decrease In Reactivity	27% Increase In Self-Awareness

Figure 13: Some Benefits of Building Your Resilience

These are just a sampling of the many benefits from building your resilience.

The 10 factors that provide you with these benefits are presented in Figure 14.

The NResilience Model®				
Focus Maintains attention to the matters & people at hand	Pragmatic Optimism Believes that the future will be better, and they will have a role in making it so	Empathy Invests in relationships by listening and being curious	Fact-Based Decision-Making Grounds assumptions, conclusions, decisions and actions in facts	Agility Quickly changes course to achieve objectives in the face of challenges
Balanced Goal-Setting Pursues measurable goals in all of life's arenas	Engaging In A Higher Purpose Connects to the greater good they serve	Self-Control Limits distractions and avoids multitasking	Grit Perseveres to achieve long-term goals	Self-Reflection Objectively reviews past behaviors, attitudes, perspectives and results to learn

Figure 14: The NResilience Model®

You don't need to develop all 10 resilience factors to get tremendous benefits and be able to thrive amid adversity. The top row of Figure 14 has the most important factors to develop in this time of uncertainty. The first three items on the top row—Focus, Pragmatic Optimism, Empathy—are what you should concentrate on first. The combined effect of these three factors will be to quell and eventually roll back your anxiety. You will rewire your brain so that your PFC will counter the amygdala emotionally hijacking you.

Once you are in control of your anxiety and other negative emotions, concentrate on building fact-based decision-making and agility. These two factors will rewire your brain to be able to cut through the tremendous perceptual overload in this environment so you can make good decisions and take effective actions.

As we discussed in Chapter 2, the latest advances in neuroscience tell us that simply practicing the behaviors related to each of these factors for 60 to 70 days actually rewires our brain to create resilient thoughts, feelings, and behaviors. In almost every case that means simply replacing a behavior that generates stress, anxiety, or depression with one that generates optimism, clarity, fulfillment, or happiness.

Here are some important things to bear in mind:

- Stick with it!
    - After about 30 days of practicing resilience-building behaviors, you will feel better. You will know you are making progress. Don't back off practicing the behaviors. For decades we've heard about 30 days to build a habit. So we've invested in countless "30-day" diets and exercise plans. We were wrong! The neuroscience clearly shows that we must consistently practice behaviors for 60 to 70 days for the rewiring of the brain to be durable and sustained.
- Be forgiving!
    - We're all imperfect human beings. We all will miss a day or two here and there of practicing our resilience behaviors. Don't let that lead to negative self-talk such as "I failed…," "I can't even do simple things…," or "What's the point of trying!" Just restart practicing the behaviors. When you forget or miss a day, forgive yourself and get back at it. I've been studying resilience for over 30 years, and I still have days when I miss a practice. Keep at it.
- Set your own pace!
    - Living in this world of uncertainty, we're all under stress and often exhausted. This book provides more than 30 different behavior sets you can practice to build your resilience. Focus on just one factor and its behaviors at a time. Don't add more until you feel comfortable practicing these behaviors consistently.

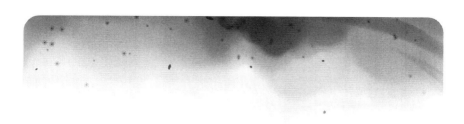

CHAPTER 4

PRAGMATIC OPTIMISM: THE FIRST FACTOR TO CONCENTRATE ON

At its core Pragmatic Optimism is the belief that the future will be better, and you will have a role in making it so. You will contribute to a better future when you do small things to make a positive difference every day. Regardless of your situation, you can build your Pragmatic Optimism as the foundation for your resilience. Overtime, you will thrive while succeeding.

As with all the chapters of this book, I'll begin with how to build the factor and then say more about why and how it works. That way you can get started building your Pragmatic Optimism right away.

The Pragmatic Optimism Routine

There are three behaviors to practice consistently to build your Pragmatic Optimism:

1. The gratitude exercise
2. Accepting the five things you cannot change
3. The three Pragmatic Optimism questions

The Gratitude Exercise

Practicing The Gratitude Exercise will allow you to sleep better and develop a neural network that builds your optimism by focusing your attention and emotions on the positive things you experience.

- Place a pad or small notebook and pen/pencil by your bedside.
- Immediately before lying down to sleep, write down five things that went well that day.

Tips

- They don't have to be "big" things. The fact that you got out for a few minutes to enjoy the sunny day, or someone paid you a compliment, or you carried out an act of kindness are all good examples of things that went well.
- Make sure you write these things down on paper—not input them into your smartphone.

That's it! Begin doing this tonight. To learn why and how this works, go to page 28.

Accepting the Five Things You Cannot Change

(Adapted from *The Five Things We Cannot Change: And the Happiness We Find by Embracing Them* by David Richo. Paperback Edition June 2006)

- There are five things that are true of everyone's life, simply because we are living a life:
    - Everything changes and ends.
    - Pain is part of life.
    - Life isn't fair.
    - Things don't go according to plan.
    - People are not loving and kind all of the time.

- Simply keep these in mind.
  - When you face a disappointment or setback or receive bad news, instead of wondering "why I deserved this" or immersing yourself in guilt or pity, remember that the primary reason we experience these five things is because they are part of everyone's life.

To learn why and how this works, go to **page 30.**

The Three Pragmatic Optimism Questions

Practice answering the following three questions whenever you are discouraged, disappointed, or feeling overwhelmed:

1. Will this (situation/circumstance) last forever?
2. Does it affect everything that is important to me in my life?
   - For example, will making a big mistake at work ruin my relationship with my family?
3. How can I use my skills, knowledge, and experiences to find a way forward?

Tips

- To be ready for a serious situation, you need to practice answering the above questions on a regular basis.
- I answer these questions when I'm stuck in traffic:
  - Will this traffic last forever?

    No, even the traffic on I-95 will eventually clear up.
  - Does it affect everything that is important to me in my life?

    No, no matter how important the meeting or event I am headed to, the impact of being late is limited to this commitment.
  - How can I use my skills, knowledge, and experiences to find a way forward?

Simple. I can call ahead—hands free—and tell folks I'll be late. Second, I can listen to a digital book to catch up on my reading.

- If you don't drive, this works equally well commuting by bus, train, or subway.

- REMEMBER: When facing a really important disappointment or setback, focus on answering these three questions.

Why and How It Works! The Gratitude Exercise

Our brains are hard-wired to remember threats to our safety. As we discussed in Chapter 2, the core of this function is the amygdala. It's an almond-shaped part of the brain in the temporal lobe of your brain. You can see its location in Figure 15. The amygdala is part of the limbic system. This system drives our emotions and impulses to survive (i.e., "fight or flight").

The amygdala perceives our emotions and remembers them and what triggered them. A major reason to remember emotions is so that we can spot similar triggers—especially those related to the emotions of fear and anxiety—so that we can respond quickly to threats.

This neurologic wiring is some of the oldest and strongest in the human brain. If you live in a part of the world where predators roam freely and place you in danger, it's very helpful to be able to quickly react to the signs of an alligator or rattlesnake.

Unfortunately, the amygdala remembers fear and anxiety related to far less lethal triggers. It remembers all those daily worries, moments of anxiousness, and mistakes. When you try to sleep at night, the amygdala forces you to keep remembering these moments and the potential danger.

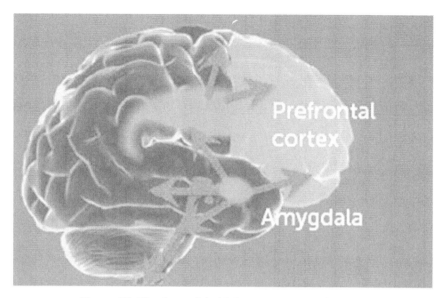

Figure 15: The Amygdala Maintaining Arousal as You
Try to Sleep Adapted From Science News

For example, "Did I really say that to my boss in that email? What's she going to say when she reads it?" "Why didn't I proofread that contract one more time before I sent it to the client?" "Did I send the prescription for Mrs. Jones to the pharmacy?" You get the idea.

The constant signaling—see Figure 15—of the amygdala to "watch out" for what has already passed prevents you from falling asleep as you toss and turn rehashing all of these "threats." The signaling also keeps you from sleeping soundly during the night so you find yourself some-times waking one or more times during the night. When you wake up in the morning, you will feel tired, sluggish, and often discouraged—without realizing why.

When you consistently write down five things that went well today, before lying down to sleep, you load your amygdala with encouraging memories. These compete with the negative memories or triggers of fear, anxiety, and other threatening emotions (see Figure 16). At the same time you are building a new neurologic path that will increase your positive emotions during the day.

Practicing the gratitude exercise will allow you to sleep better and develop a neural network that builds your optimism by focusing your attention and emotions on the positive things you experience.

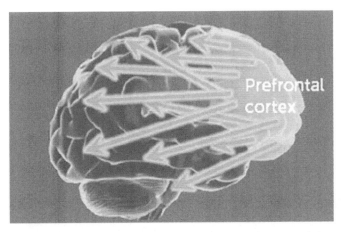

Figure 16: The Prefrontal Cortex Countering the Amygdala's Efforts to Maintain Arousal Adapted From Science News

Accepting the Five Things You Cannot Change

The core neurologic principle that serves as our foundation for developing resilience is that anything experienced consistently over time (usually a maximum of 70 days) will cause your brain to create a circuit, making that thinking, feeling, or behavior your automatic response to similar situations.

Many of us have experienced things consistently in life that have created neural circuits that trigger feelings of guilt and self-blame on a quite frequent basis. For example, consider the parents of a child with a chronic or life-threatening illness who can't find a clear cause of why their child developed this illness. Driven by the brain's need to make sense of the world (the need for closure), these parents will often start to blame themselves and each other. The blaming can become constant—often to the point of interfering with the parents' ability to clearly and effectively manage the child's illness. The blaming conversation can also destroy the parents' relationship.

Here's another example. Consider the child who was verbally abused growing up, always being told they were a failure or not good enough and perhaps consistently compared with others and told, "Why can't you be like your brother/sister?" This constant negative abuse can wire the child's brain to feel guilt and low self-esteem in the face of any perceived failure.

Remembering the five things we cannot change challenges our automatic feelings of guilt, self-doubt, and worthlessness when we start to think or say things such as:

- "What did I do to deserve this?"
- "Why does my child have to suffer from this illness?"
- "This isn't fair. Why am I suffering in this way?"
- "Maybe if only I had _____ this wouldn't have happened."

Consistently reviewing the five things we cannot change over time will build a healthy, automatic response to life's disappointments, challenges, and heartbreaks. "What did I do to deserve this?" will automatically be followed by "I did nothing to deserve this. Life isn't fair for anyone. Pain is part of everyone's life. I should have handled the situation better, but I don't deserve to continually suffer because I made a mistake. Making mistakes is a natural part of life. I need to apologize for and learn from my mistakes. Then move on."

Again, the key is to review the five things we cannot change on a regular basis to build a healthy, neurologic and emotional response to life's disappointments and frustrations.

The Three Pragmatic Optimism Questions

For many people, when something bad happens they experience three emotional reactions. These reactions happen quickly, often simultaneously, and can quickly overwhelm us. They can feel like tremendous waves hitting you all at once, interfering with your ability to breathe, take in information, or see a way forward.

These waves wash over you, making you feel like the turmoil and uncertainty will last forever, you will lose everything, and there is nothing you can do to save yourself.

If you've grown up swimming in the ocean, you know what this feels like. If you've been properly trained, you also know that rough waters don't last forever; while you feel threatened, you're not going to lose everything, and there are specific things you can do to get out of trouble:

- Don't panic.
- If you're being dragged out away from shore, swim parallel to the shore until you break free of the current.

Let's look at another example. You are called in to meet with your boss and someone from Human Resources (HR). Your job has been eliminated so you are being laid off. The HR professional explains what severance, benefits, and outplacement services you will receive. You absorb very little, if any, of the information provided because you are overwhelmed by three emotional reactions:

- "This is the end of my career. I'll never find another job."
- "This is going to ruin my life. I can't tell my spouse/partner. They love me for what I do in supporting them."
- "I have no idea what to do next."

Because of these emotional reactions, you may begin to panic or shut down.

You also miss the very important information that you are not being laid off for another 60 days (under certain circumstances this is required by federal law). You don't catch that you will get one week of severance pay for every year you've worked for the company. For you, that means 10 weeks of pay. Taken together, you won't have to worry about money for four and a half months, which doesn't include unemployment benefits. Not hearing this information adds to your sense of pessimism about your situation.

You have a choice. Those emotional reactions were wired in your brain by past experiences. If you consistently practice the three Pragmatic Optimism questions, this old wiring will actually be deleted by your brain and replaced by new, more realistic, and optimistic responses.

Let's take another look at the meeting with your boss and HR, after you've been consistently practicing the three Pragmatic Optimism questions.

Boss: "The company is eliminating your position. You will be laid off in 60 days."

Your Thoughts: "This is bad news. It won't last forever, and it won't start for 60 days. I've got time to plan."

HR: "The company is providing one week of severance for every year you've worked here. For you, that's 10 weeks of severance pay. In addition, you'll be eligible to keep your healthcare benefits under COBRA for 18 months following your last day of employment."

Your Thoughts: "Ok. Everything is not going to be impacted by this. When I tell my husband, he'll be relieved to hear we'll still have healthcare coverage and it will be four and a half months before we have to live on less. With unemployment benefits we'll have even more time."

Boss: "We know this is a shock. Take some time to think things through. Next week HR and an outplacement firm will start offering workshops to help you find your next job."

Your Thoughts: "I've been here 10 years, which has given me a lot of new skills and accomplishments. I can apply my experience and skills to find another job. It's not like it was 10 years ago when I had little experience. I can work through this."

The key is that to have an optimistic, healthy response to a setback or bad news, you have to build your neural circuit to automatically respond with the three Pragmatic Optimism questions. Practice responding to minor disappointments and setbacks by answering these three questions. When you can't get a reservation for your anniversary dinner at your favorite restaurant, answer these three questions. When you're stuck in traffic or your flight is delayed, answer these three questions. That's how you build a new and healthy neural circuit.

Again, the three Pragmatic Optimism questions are:

1. Will this (situation/circumstance) last forever?
2. Does it affect everything that is important to me in my life?
3. How can I use my skills, knowledge, and experiences to find a way forward?

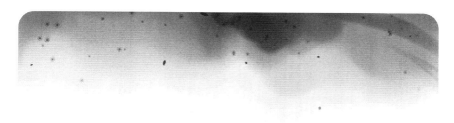

CHAPTER 5

FOCUS

F ocus is the ability to maintain your attention on the things you want to concentrate on—to keep your thoughts, emotions, and behaviors centered on the matters and people at hand. Focus enables you to block out the distractions of the "always on world" and to work on high priority objectives for extended periods of time.

Focus is an essential foundation of resilience for everyone in today's world.

As with all our chapters, I'll begin with how to build the factor and then say more about why and how it works. That way you can get started building your resilience right away.

The Focus Routine

There are five behaviors to practice consistently to build your Focus:

1. The 20-minute breathing meditation
2. The three-minute breathing meditation
3. The cleansing breath
4. Arriving mindfully
5. Scheduling for focus

The first three of the above behaviors involve breathing. Let's review how to properly breath before we go into each of these three behaviors.

Proper Breathing

The most effective way of breathing—especially when we are under stress or anxious— is called diaphragmatic or belly breathing. It ensures we take full deep breaths and maximize our intake of oxygen to supply our brain and our body. The following checklist walks you through this breathing.

Belly Breathing

- Close your eyes or gaze softly at a point six or so feet away.
- Notice how you are breathing.
- Breathe through your nose.
- Put one hand below your belly button.
- Put your other hand at the center of your upper chest.
- Inhale as you expand your belly out and feel your hand rising.
- Exhale and feel your belly go flat—like a balloon flattening.

Practice diaphragmatic (belly) breathing when you do all of the meditation exercises.

The 20-Minute Breathing Meditation

- Find a quiet place where you can sit comfortably for 20 minutes.
- Sit straight without being rigid.
- Close your eyes if you feel comfortable or gaze softly at a point 10 to15 feet in front of you.
- Notice where you feel your breathing most clearly.
    - o That may be in your belly, in your chest, or at your lips or nostrils.
    - o Just pick the place where you feel your breathing the most.

- Now simply focus your attention on your breathing.
  - As you breathe in, think to yourself, "Breathing in, I know I am breathing in," then "Breathing out, I know I am breathing out."
- Continue for 20 minutes.
- Do this once a day.

Tips

- Our mind wanders naturally so don't be discouraged by thoughts or feelings that emerge.
  - Simply, and without self-criticism, refocus your attention on your breathing when you notice your mind has wondered.
  - It is bringing your attention back to your breathing after it wanders that is the most powerful part of meditating.
- If you're really struggling and getting frustrated, stop!
  - Come back and try again later.
- Sometimes you will fall asleep or feel like you are waking up when meditating. That's ok.
  - It simply means either you are not getting enough sleep or that you have been tightly wound so the relaxation of meditation allows you to sleep.
- It is often a good idea to do this at the same time each day.
- Many people do it first thing in the morning.

The Three-Minute Breathing Meditation

This is the same as the 20-minute breathing meditation with the following differences:

- It is much shorter.
- You can do it in any quiet spot.
  - People who drive to work may go sit in the car for three minutes.
  - Others find a quiet bench outside.

o   If you have an office, just close the door.

o   You should do these three times a day.

o   It is a powerful way of improving your focus just before an important meeting or presentation.

o   You should do it whenever you are feeling overwhelmed or especially distracted.

o   It is also a powerful way of transitioning from home to work and then work to home.

   ▪   Do it before entering your workplace.

   ▪   Do it just before entering your home.

Again, the routine is the same as the 20-minute breathing meditation:

- Sit straight without being rigid.
- Close your eyes if you feel comfortable or gaze softly at a point 10 to15 feet in front of you.
- Notice where you feel your breathing most clearly.
   o   That may be in your belly, in your chest, or at your lips or nostrils.
   o   Just pick the place where you feel your breathing the most.
- Now simply focus your attention on your breathing.
   o   As you breathe in, think to yourself, "Breathing in, I know I am breathing in," then "Breathing out, I know I am breathing out."
- Continue for three minutes.

The Cleansing Breath

Use this very short technique when you are feeling stress and anxiety rise. Also use it when you feel you are about to enter into a conflict. The following checklist guides you through this simple, yet powerful, technique.

1.   Inhale deeply through your nose, expanding your belly.
2.   Exhale through puckered lips.

3. Let your head drop to your chest as you exhale.
4. Repeat four or five times.

Arriving Mindfully

The objective of this behavior is to fully switch your focus from one activity to another. For example, switch from writing an email to making/answering a phone call or from walking down the hall thinking about a project to entering the room to attend a meeting.

The practice is elegant. It is merely taking 15 to 30 seconds to allow your senses to anchor you in the new environment. It's a simple, yet powerful, way of making sure you fully shift from one setting and agenda to the next.

- When entering a new environment or switching tasks, simply pause to sit or stand still without talking for 15 to 30 seconds.
- Make a mental note of the transition you are making.
  - o I am going to call Jim to discuss...
  - o I am going into the team meeting.
- Note what you see; look all around.
- Note what you hear; attend to subtle sounds.
- Note what you feel in terms of temperature/climate and in terms of emotion.

Scheduling for Focus

How you schedule and manage your time can make a huge improvement in your ability to focus and get things done. There are six key changes in how you organize your time that will make a significant difference in your productivity and quality of work. Most importantly, it will make you feel more fulfilled.

1. Don't look at your smartphone before your first hour of work.
   - Many people keep their smartphone by the bedside. It's the first thing they grab in the morning.
   - Before their feet hit the bedroom floor, they are overwhelmed and distracted.
2. Spend your first 55 minutes of each day on your highest priority.
   - In today's world it is no longer possible to be someone who is more productive in the afternoon, evening, or late night.
   - The first 55 minutes are your most productive.
3. After 55 minutes spend 10 minutes on nonwork.
   - Meditate.
   - Read the newspaper.
   - Take a walk.
4. Establish huddles three times a day.
   - If you manage people and find them interrupting you throughout the day, establish three huddle times.
   - A huddle is a period of 10 to 15 minutes when you will be available to share information and give support to your people.
   - Set three huddle periods a day.
   - For example, 8:40 a.m. to 8:55 a.m. (assuming you spend 7:30 a.m. – 8:25 a.m. on your most important priority of the day), 11:40 a.m. to 11:55 a.m., and 4:15 p.m. to 4:30 p.m.
5. Here are the huddle rules:
   - If you come to a huddle, I will share any news I have, tell you what I've done to help you, and hear what new assistance you may need.
   - After each huddle I'm scheduled to focus on work critical to our team's success. I won't be free until the next huddle.
   - If you miss a huddle, that's ok.
   - The next time I'll be available to help you is our next huddle.
   - If you have something that is truly urgent and important, then come see me in person or call me on the phone.
   - Don't email, text, or instant message.

Tips

- Some people may intentionally try to "break" you and get back to the old ways of interrupting your day—and theirs!
  - o If they show up one minute after the huddle ended, tell them you look forward to seeing them at the next huddle.
  - o If they have a true emergency that can't be delayed, tell them "I'm disappointed you didn't get to the huddle so we could address this."
- Two of the most powerful words to set boundaries for people are "disappointed" and "unacceptable."
  - o Simply saying "I'm disappointed that you..." or "That is unacceptable" are very powerful ways of letting people know they are crossing the line.
- After you make one of the above statements, do not engage in conversation. Don't allow the person to start a debate.

6. Make a supportive deferral.

If you have people stopping by your workspace or office or constantly instant messaging, this is how to regain control over your time.

- First, turn off your email or instant messaging—just for 55-minute blocks.
- Let people know that in an emergency they can get hold of you on your smartphone.
- Now when someone "drops by" or calls on your cell phone:
  - o Say: "Leo, I'm working on something really important right now. Truthfully, if I stopped to talk to you now, I would be distracted by it. I'm sure what you want me to discuss requires my full attention. You deserve my full attention. So let's meet at _____. I'll be clear-headed and fully focused on helping you."
  - o If the person insists on speaking to you, they are unintentionally acknowledging that what they want to talk about doesn't require your full attention (unless there's

a true emergency such as "We've just experienced a cyberattack"). So why do they have to interrupt you now?[6]

7. Schedule overflow time.

You know that during your day "crises" will occur. You don't know what they will be or when they will happen. The real problem is that you don't budget time in your calendar for them. So when they do occur such as important priorities that require you working late into the night or weekends, here's the solution.

- Each week block out four to six hours of time.
- Usually two-hour blocks work best.
- Don't allow anyone to book meetings on your calendar in these blocks.
- If you have to book something in one of these blocks, simultaneously book another "overflow" time the same week.
- Now when a crisis occurs, you have space in your calendar so you can immediately move whatever you had scheduled when the crisis occurred to an overtime slot.
- In a meeting you can immediately say to the other attendees: "I have time during these three blocks this week."
- If working on a document or managing your dashboard, you immediately reschedule that task to the next "overflow" time.

Why and How It Works!
Diaphragmatic (Belly) Breathing

When we are under stress or feeling anxious, we tend to:

- Take very shallow breaths using only the very top portion of our lungs
- Shorten our inhaling
- Not fully exhale
- Use only the muscles in our upper chest

The result is we don't maximize the amount of oxygen we inhale and the amount of carbon dioxide we exhale, which reduces the amount of oxygen in our blood stream, interfering with our brain and body function. The lack of oxygen triggers or increases anxiety. Muscles tighten throughout our body, again increasing feelings of stress and anxiety.

The diaphragm is designed to expand downward when we inhale to maximize our intake of oxygen and to contract upward to when we exhale to maximize our discharge of carbon monoxide. When we only use the muscles in our upper chest, the diaphragm can't perform these functions.

When we diaphragmatically breathe, we fully enable the diaphragm to fulfill its functions. Our blood, body, and brain are oxygen enriched, which triggers a relaxation response that relaxes muscles throughout the body. Our prefrontal cortex becomes more effective. We can take control of our fear and anxiety. We can concentrate, take in and analyze information, develop choices, and act effectively.

The 20-Minute Breathing Meditation

Any experience we consistently repeat will rewire our brains. In today's world of 24/7 overload, we are constantly experiencing distractions and interruptions. As a result, our brains become neurologically wired to be hyper-responsive to any stimulus—be it the ping of an incoming text, a pop-up notification on our tablet, or the ability to do an unimportant Google search while at your laptop.

Meditation builds two neural networks or wirings. First, we build the network that increases our ability to maintain our attention where we want it. Second, we build the network that enables us to quickly recover from distractions. As we meditate, the first network will increase the length of time we can stay focused on the task in front of us. Even more importantly, as you meditate your thoughts and feelings will continue to distract you from focusing on your breath. As soon as you realize you are being distracted you will bring your attention back to your breathing, which builds the second neural circuit. As with any neural networks, these become more and more powerful over time. In the case of recovering from distractions, you will become better and better at not being drawn away by thoughts and feelings. When you are drawn away, you will refocus more quickly.

After eight weeks of meditation, brain imaging shows significant changes in brain density in areas related to:

- Working memory
- Perception
- Decision-making
- Social interaction
- Emotional control[7]

In brain images (see Figure 17), the shaded areas show where the brain density has increased. The brain is encased in the skull so it cannot grow in size. We measure its power by the density of the cells within the brain. Much like a computer chip, the higher the density of the connections, the more powerful the chip or the brain.

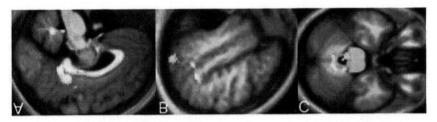

Figure 17: Brain Images Highlighting Areas of Increased Brain Density Hölzel, B.K., Carmody, J., Vangel, M., Congleton C., Yerramsetti, S.M., Gard, T, & Lazar, S.W. (2011)."Mindfulness practice leads to increases in regional brain gray matter density." Psychiatry Res. 191(1): 36-43.

In the same study, researchers measured the brain density of people before and after they began an eight-week program of meditation. The study showed that the density of brain tissue increased between the beginning and end of the program.

In sum, we have hard neurological evidence that meditation physically increases the power of our brain.

The study also showed a decrease in the brain density of the control subjects. Control subjects are people whose brain scans were taken but did not participate in the eight-week meditation program. What this proves is that when people do not meditate, the experience of living in today's world of continuous stimulus overload can erode our brain and decrease its functioning.

> *"Meditation allows us to practice mindfulness. Mindfulness is the awareness that emerges through paying attention, on purpose, in the present moment, and nonjudgmentally, to things as they are."*
>
> —*Williams, Teasdale, Segal, & Kabat-Zinn (2007)*[8]

In other words, in whatever situation we find ourselves we can be fully present, which is critical to thriving in the thin air of today's world. It allows you to concentrate and process the information that your mind breathes in—just as mountain climbers need to more efficiently draw in oxygen as they go higher and higher into thin air.

Is being present important? Critically so. Your productivity depends on it. Your happiness and ability to thrive depend on it.

Harvard psychologists Matthew Killingsworth and Daniel Gilbert did a study[9] that determined not being present in the moment is a major cause of unhappiness. When you are present and engaged in what is in front of you, you are happier and more fulfilled.

In the same study they found that people are distracted 47 percent of the time. Think about that. Suppose you are in a 30-minute conversation. You are not present 47 percent of the time, and the other person is not present 47 percent of the time. And your presence—or lack thereof—is not correlated. It's possible you might both be present at the same time as little as five minutes out of 30 minutes.

Here's another important implication. When we are distracted and not present, our brain is on auto fire. As soon as your brain perceives a stimulus, it fires off a response. Often you don't even realize you are responding before you finish.

S ➡ R

Figure 18: Belief That Stimulus Immediately Leads To A Response

You hear the ping of a text and automatically open it. Perhaps you have an emotional response to what appears and fire off an inappropriate response. Digital conflict ensues!

The famous psychiatrist Victor Frankel pointed out: "Between the stimulus and the response there is a space. In that space is our power to choose our response. In our response lies our growth and freedom."[10]

If you build your brain's neural capacity to focus and minimize distractions, you realize there is a very brief awareness of what you are about to do before responding. If you capture that awareness, you can control your response.

Figure 19: Knowledge That Awareness Exists Between Stimulus and Response

Imagine how many mistakes and misunderstandings you can avoid just by seeing and using that "A" between the "S" and the "R."

The Three-Minute Breathing Meditation

Practicing the three-minute breathing meditation is similar to practicing the 20-minute breathing meditation with a couple of important differences.

The three-minute breathing meditation is not long enough to build strong, durable neural networks in your brain. That's why practicing the 20-minute breathing meditation is necessary to build focus.

The three-minute breathing meditation is a very powerful way of accessing the focus neural networks you have and are building.

For many of us, the day starts with many demands: demands to get partners/spouses, parents, and children off to their day; perceived demands to answer overnight texts and emails immediately; and getting yourself organized and out the door to work, school, or both. The number of demands and distractions we experience just keeps multiplying as the day goes on. In response, many of us resort to multitasking.

The part of your brain that is critical to understanding and analyzing things, comparing information or alternatives, and then making decisions is called the prefrontal cortex. As shown in Figure 20, the prefrontal cortex is located right behind the forehead. It is also one of the newest parts of your brain to evolve.

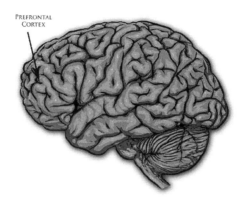

Figure 20: Prefrontal Cortex From: Medium.Com

The prefrontal cortex uses a lot of energy and has a limited capacity. When we multitask, we try to process more information in the prefrontal cortex than it can manage.

For example, you are writing an important email to your boss. She needs it for a meeting with her boss. Time is tight, and you are scheduled to join a conference call. You don't want to be late so you sign in to the conference call. You continue writing the email while you try to listen to the call and participate when you are expected to. Next, an instant message pops up on your screen. You "read" it while continuing to listen to the call and deciding what to write next in the email.

You have loaded three separate tasks requiring attention to new information, analysis of new information, and generating new information. The prefrontal cortex does not process all three tasks simultaneously. It switches back and forth from one to the next. The switching is unrelated to how important a task is at any given moment.

Here's a true example. I was speaking on resilience at a meeting sponsored by The Conference Board. I had just finished the section on focus and multitasking. We took a break, and a vice president from one of the sponsoring companies came up to me. She said, "I wish you had been here yesterday!" I was a little puzzled by that comment. so I said, "Really. Tell me more."

"Yesterday I was in the exact situation you described. Writing an email to my boss, listening in on a conference call, and staying on top of emails. The conference call was with a task force I've been on for 18 months. We've been asking for funds for 16 months. The task force leader announced we had finally gotten the funds. My response was "That's wonderful!"

Too soon I interrupted, "Well, after 16 months it sure was! Congratulations!"

She responded, "Well, thanks. Unfortunately, at the same time the funding was announced I had an email open announcing that a senior executive—who's very difficult to work with—is leaving for family reasons. I didn't say "That's wonderful!" into the phone. I typed it, including an exclamation mark in my response to the email about the senior executive leaving. And, of course, I hit Reply All."

In a nutshell what happened was her prefrontal cortex heard the good news about funding and switched to the email at the exact point in time when it was generating the response to the good news. Literally, her neurologic wires got crossed.

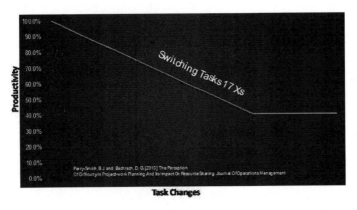

Figure 21: Impact of Multitasking on Productivity

Another problem with trying to multitask is that every time you switch tasks your productivity drops by 3.5%[11]—until you hit a floor of 40 percent productivity. You only have to switch tasks 17 times to hit that floor (see Figure 21).

So multitasking significantly reduces our productivity at work.

Here's another interesting finding: Researchers at the University of London assessed people's IQs before and after multitasking. They found that multitasking dropped a person's working IQ an average of 15 points. That put them at the cognitive capacity of an eight-year-old.[12]

Now here's the really good news: If you do nothing you will have those productivity and cognitive deficits all day. However, if you practice the three-minute breathing meditation, you reset your brain. You reverse the productivity and cognitive deficits.

I recommend you practice the three-minute breathing meditation three or more times each day. Practice whenever you start to feel like your brain is trying to work at warp speed or you realize you have been multitasking or there is just "too much going on." It takes just three minutes to reset the brain and retake control.

Arriving Mindfully

If you read the previous section, you know how much multitasking and distractions during your day cost you in productivity and cognitive function. Arriving mindfully purposely switches your thoughts and emotions from what you have been doing to the environment you are entering or task you are about to begin.

When you practice arriving mindfully, you intentionally trigger the brain's networks that "turn off" what you are thinking about and "dampen down" any strong emotions you may be feeling. You are intentionally throwing the switch for these neural networks.

For example, you are signaling the amygdala to let go of any strong emotions it is stimulating. You are signaling the prefrontal cortex to clear itself of all other thoughts, analysis, and decision-making it is involved in before you enter a new situation.

Have you ever walked into a meeting distracted? Maybe you were even reading text messages on your smartphone? You find yourself taken by surprise when the meeting actually starts. You're further surprised when three of the people at the meeting immediately begin to angrily argue. Maybe without even realizing why you become angry and join in the fray.

That happens because you are multitasking so you are not taking in the meeting environment. You are not noticing body language or the tone of the pre-meeting conversation. You become angry simply because the amygdala—having no other data—takes the angry conversation as a threat to you. So it responds with "fight." If instead of joining in you find yourself unusually quiet and shut down, it's because your amygdala has chosen the "flight" response. You can't physically leave the meeting so you try to fade into the background.

If instead of walking in distracted you practiced arriving mindfully, you would have taken in all the information available in the room—the tone of the group. Is the group unusually quiet? Is the group unusually loud? Split into cliques? You would notice the body language and tone of all the individuals.

All this information is processed by a clear amygdala and prefrontal cortex. You respond based on information in a clear way that gives you the best advantage.

Remember this: In neurologic terms, a strong emotion always beats logic. If you don't clear your amygdala and prefrontal cortex, your behavior will be driven by emotions—perhaps inappropriate ones.[13]

Scheduling For Focus

How you schedule and manage your time can make a tremendous improvement in your ability to focus and get things done. To review, there are six key changes in how you organize your time that will make a meaningful increase in both the amount and quality of your productivity. Most importantly, it will make you feel more fulfilled.

1. Don't look at your smartphone before your first hour of work.
2. Spend your first 55 minutes of each day on your highest priority.
3. After 55 minutes, spend 10 minutes on nonwork.
4. Establish huddles three times a day.
5. Use the supportive deferral.
6. Schedule overflow time.

Don't Look at Your Smartphone Before Your First Hour of Work

Earlier I reviewed the fact that when multitasking, every time you switch tasks your productivity drops by 3.5 percent.[14]—until you hit a floor of 40 percent productivity. You only have to switch tasks 17 times to hit that floor.

So if your smartphone is by your bed and you pick it up and start looking at your emails, newsfeeds, and texts, you can easily switch tasks 17+ times—before your feet hit the floor! You start the day 60 percent less productive.

A friend of mine is an attorney. When I explained this, he responded, "You don't understand. Our clients expect an immediate response to any of their requests. I have to respond as soon as I wake up."

Up to a challenge, I asked, "What time do you get up?"

"Five a.m. sharp."

"And your clients know that?"

He smiled as he got my point. His clients don't know whether he gets up at 5 a.m., 6 a.m., or another time.

Spend Your First 55 Minutes of Each Day on Your Highest Priority After 55 Minutes Spend 10 Minutes on Nonwork

There was a time when people would say they were most productive in the afternoon, early evening, or in the wee hours of the night. That time is over. We all try to breathe in the digital deluge.[15] The constant, overwhelming firehose of input, digital, and otherwise. So the time when all of us can be the most productive and achieve the highest quality based on the best decisions is our first hour of work each day.

Any time after that first hour your brain has been assaulted and deficits incurred by the environment we all breathe in.

Why 55 minutes? Research has shown that the top 10 percent of people, in terms of productivity, spend 52 minutes working, followed by a 17-minute break doing nonwork.[16] I've taken the liberty of rounding the numbers for convenience.

Establish Huddles Three Times a Day

As I previously reviewed, a huddle is just a 10- to15-minute period when you are available to your team and they are available to you. The purpose is to share information and make new requests for support or decisions.

If you manage even one person, being interrupted by those you lead is a major source of distraction, most often in the form of multitasking. People distract you by showing up at your cubicle or office door without appointments. Or they constantly email, text, or instant message you—and sometimes they use all three forms of interruption (you really can't call these forms of communication). Always with an "urgent" matter!

Here are the top five things you probably note once you hear what the "urgent" matter is:

1. They've come to you without getting as much information as possible.
2. They haven't developed some options for addressing the problem.
3. They clearly have the authority to handle this matter on their own.
4. The "urgent" matter could have waited four hours or longer to be addressed.
5. The solution was pretty obvious once they just took a breath (or practiced arriving mindfully or a three-minute breathing meditation).

So here's how huddles reduce and eventually eliminate distractions. First, the obvious. You are consistently available to your people three times a day—and usually less than four hours from the moment they become aware of the "urgent" matter.

To interrupt you instead of waiting for a huddle sends one or more of the following messages to you (my boss) and my coworkers:

- I don't have respect for my boss's operating rules.

- I can't calmly and effectively move forward on an "urgent" matter while I'm waiting for my boss to approve my decision.
- I think my work is more important than anyone else's.
- I appear some combination of disorganized, overwhelmed, and anxious.

When you use huddles, these messages are in the person's mind as they start to create an email, text, or instant message or pick up the phone or come see you in person. Their awareness of those messages causes them to pause. They decide to delay reaching out to you—first, for a minute or two, to think things through and then until the next huddle. Finally, they decide to gather more information and come up with some potential options. Maybe they even solve the problem.

I was consulting to an IT organization in a prominent global bank. They had come to me because they knew that the entire organization was experiencing some level of burnout. Given the demands on the teams, things weren't going to be any less demanding for quite some time. In addition to the burnout, over 85% of IT projects were over budget, extremely late, or failing to meet the businesses needs. In some cases, all three.

About 75 people worked in one open plan office. People had their workspaces side by side. All the managers were in the last workspace on the right side of a row. We chose to launch our resilience building intervention with an intensive, one-day working session. The session was held in a glass walled conference room looking out on the open plan office. We then followed the working session with coaching the managers in groups of four for an hour every week.

Two weeks after the working session, I found myself in the same conference room doing small group coaching sessions. In between sessions I would have a 10- to 15-minute break. As I looked out into the workspace, I was able to watch people change their behavior in the midst of working under intense pressure. Over and over again, I saw people get up from their workstation and start to walk down the row to their boss. As they walked along, they would slow down, stop, think for a minute, then return to their workstation. I then watched these same people be the first to arrive for the next huddle with their manager and to quickly engage with the manager.

Later I spoke to a number of team members and several of the managers.

Here's what one of the team members said:

> *I'm used to running down the row with a problem. It's like you said: It's hard-wired. That's why I got up. As I was moving toward my manager, I tried that arriving mindfully thing. I saw how busy my manager was. I could see she was multitasking like crazy. Honestly, I was afraid if I jumped into what she was trying to handle, it wouldn't be good for me. So I turned around and went back to my workstation to wait for the next huddle. The next huddle was almost three hours away. It would look bad if I came to the huddle with a problem I had stewed on for more than three hours without making any progress. I spent about half of the three hours getting more information and talking to the people most impacted by the problem. Then I used that agility tool you showed us and came to the huddle with several pretty good solutions.*

Here's what the person's manager said:

> *One of the things I learned about myself is that part of me actually liked being interrupted by my team. It made me feel important—even indispensable. And usually their problems were easier for me to solve than the one's on my plate. That realization made me more committed to making the huddles work.*
>
> *All day long I see people start toward me and then stop and turn around. As time goes by, fewer and fewer people are even beginning to come to me.*
>
> *When we have a huddle, they present problems calmly and logically. Almost always they've laid out a few viable solutions. More and more they have taken action to solve the problem and are just bringing me up to speed.*

*With far fewer interruptions I'm getting way more done,
and I'm not as fried at the end of the day. My team is also
getting more done and feeling a greater sense of accomplishment.*

The bottom line: Huddles increase the productivity of your entire team.

The Supportive Deferral

You've just told your team that you're establishing huddles to minimize distractions and interruptions for everyone. You've been clear about the three times a day when the huddles will take place. So why should you be prepared for one or more of these same people to continue to interrupt you?

This is another case where a strong emotion trumps logic. First, when you ask people to change, you trigger strong emotions. As the best-selling book *Who Moved My Cheese?*[17] illustrated, these can be triggered by even relatively minor changes. These emotions drive a response contrary to what you requested.

Second, resisting new management policies and procedures is a learned behavior. Learned behaviors are hard-wired. In this particular case the wiring may drive clear resistance—resistance that in the past has proven to work.

A few illustrations. A European convenience store chain of about 500 stores decided to heavily invest in improving customer service. The Executive Committee (EC) made benchmarking trips across Europe, the United States, and Canada. Based on their strategic goals, competitive analysis, and benchmarking, they put in place a new customer service system to drive culture change. The system included the definition of a branded customer experience, new hiring practices, more training in customer service, coaching and performance management at the store level, and a new store manager's dashboard.

The company held a first-ever leadership conference for all 500 store managers to announce the new strategy and provide some initial store manager training.

Two weeks later, the EC began visiting the stores—all of the stores. About 100 store managers—or 20 percent—were completely on board with the new strategy and generating excitement and sales in their stores. About 60 percent were struggling to get it going and anxious to make it work. The remaining 100 store managers were headed in the opposite direction. They were not increasing the number of hours associates worked during peak times. They were still personally focused on inventory, merchandise, and loss prevention—and not spending any more time serving customers. Finally, from what the EC could tell, they had gone from spending little time coaching associates to almost no time coaching and reverting to a "command and control" style.

Fortunately, the EC had expected these responses. An EC member sat down with each of the 100 resistors and listened to their objections to the strategy. Where there was a misunderstanding, they clarified the strategy. Where there was cynicism, the EC member provided data supporting the strategy and reviewed "What's in It for Me" (WIIFM) with the store manager. Where the store manager had discovered a real limitation to the strategy, the EC member acknowledged and committed to trying to resolve it over time. The EC member ended the conversation by setting the expectation that the store manager would fully execute the strategy.

After three such conversations, over three months, 50 resisting store managers were terminated. That's how powerful learned resistance can be—people will lose their jobs even when encouraged and supported to change.

The good news is six months after the strategy was in place, revenues were up 10 percent. Six months later they were up 17 percent. A full 60 percent of shoppers gave the chain the highest loyalty scores. The share price tripled.

The point is you have to expect 10 to 20 percent of any group of people to follow their emotions, such as cynicism, to resist even the soundest, most logical request for change.

The supportive deferral is a tactic you should expect to use. You expect people to resist your change. So when it does happen, you are not surprised or angry. You are ready to handle it calmly, consistently, and effectively.

When you anticipate and respond calmly to resistance, you maintain control. You send a clear signal—without threatening—that the change you've requested will occur.

Schedule Overflow Time

This technique works because it keeps you in control. You don't feel trapped when the unexpected occurs. You know you have blocks of time when you can shift tasks without working until midnight. Being able to shift things keeps you calmer, prevents burnout from working too many hours, and sends a signal to those around you that everything can be handled well without entering crisis mode.

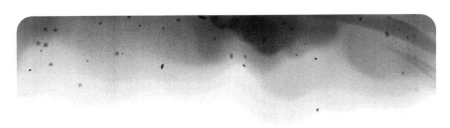

CHAPTER 6

BUILDING EMPATHY

Building empathy is investing in relationships so that you can see a situation from someone else's point of view. Perhaps most importantly, you can understand and share the feelings they have about the problem, challenge, or situation they face.

As with all our chapters, I'll begin with how to build the factor and then say more about why and how it works. That way you can get started building your resilience right away.

The Routine

There are five techniques to practice consistently to strengthen building empathy:

1. Loving kindness
2. The empathic conversation
3. The BATHE technique
4. The positive BATHE technique
5. Inclusive word choice

Loving Kindness

When you are encountering someone with whom you want to develop an empathetic relationship, think to yourself in regard to them:

- May you be safe.
- May you be healthy.
- May you be happy.
- May you live with ease.
- May you live with purpose.

Next, think those same things with regard to yourself:

- May I be safe.
- May I be healthy.
- May I be happy.
- May I live with ease.
- May I live with purpose.

The Empathic Conversation

The empathic conversation has the following five behaviors:

1. Be curious: Ask questions.
2. Listen intently—to words, tone, and body language.
3. Acknowledge what you hear: Let people know what they said means to you.
4. Stay open: Don't interrupt or shut down when you hear things you don't agree with.
5. Be yourself: Be comfortable talking about you.

The empathic conversation is not a quick "How are you?" and "move on" conversation. In fact, when well done, it is a series of conversations. The empathic conversation provides a general framework for having conversations that can build empathy.

Tips

- Be intentional by creating a list of people you want to have strong relationships with.
- Don't rush it.

- Have at least some of these conversations "off the grid"—in a relaxed atmosphere where you won't be interrupted.
- Don't look at your smartphone. Don't even have your smartphone visible!
- Be prepared to hear things you don't agree with or don't like—and don't judge the person for these viewpoints or feelings.
- Use these five behaviors in your normal meetings and conversations.

The BATHE Technique

The BATHE technique uses four questions followed by a statement(s) in a specific order:

1. BACKGROUND: "What are the things that are going on for you?"
2. AFFECT: "How do you feel about it?"
3. TROUBLES: "What troubles you the most?"
4. HOW: "How are you handling these situations?"
5. EMPATHY: Convey understanding.
   - Reflect back what things are important to the individual about their situation, how they feel about them, and what they are doing to move forward.

Tips

- Use this technique to build empathy with someone who is in a difficult situation.
- Sometimes a BATHE conversation will only take a few minutes.
  - o Don't push the person deeper or longer than they are comfortable.
  - o Be prepared for a long conversation should the person want to engage in one.
- Ask the questions as written
  - o "How are things?" doesn't focus on the person; it focuses on how they see the situation.

o   "How are you?" focuses on the person.

  ▪   It may make you seem intrusive or naive.

The Positive BATHE Technique[18]

The positive BATHE technique uses four questions followed by a state-ment(s) in a specific order:

1. BEST: "What's the best thing that has happened to you this week?" or "What's the best thing that has happened to you since we last saw each other?"
2. AFFECT: "How did that make you feel?" or "How do you account for that?"
3. THANKFULNESS: "For what are you most thankful?"
4. HAPPENED: "How can you make things like that happen more often?"
5. EMPOWERMENT: "That sounds great. I believe you can do that."

Tip

• Use the positive BATHE technique when you have already used the BATHE technique and sense the person needs support in moving forward.

Inclusive Word Choice

There are two simple behaviors to build empathy through inclusive word choice:

• Increase the use of the words us, we, our, and ourselves.
• Decrease the use of the words I, me, my, and myself.

Tips

• Be authentic in increasing your use of inclusive words.

- You are not just switching out words; you are changing the way you think about work and working with others.
- For a deeper understanding of the power of word choice, read James W. Pennebaker's *The Secret Life of Pronouns*.[19]

Why and How It Works!

First, let's define empathy. Empathy is the ability to take someone's perspective on what they are experiencing. There are two parts to empathy: (1) Cognitive empathy is the set of facts the person is selecting from all the facts, analyzing, and acting on; and (2) emotional empathy is how the person feels about the experience. When you are empathetic you can see the person's experience through the facts they focus on and the emotions they feel.

Sympathy is simply understanding that someone is having a bad experience and knowing that if it were you, you would feel badly.

Compassion is empathy combined with the desire to do something about the other person's experience—in other words, to help them.

Here are some examples of the use and power of empathy techniques. Hurricane Sandy hit the Northeast Coast of the United States on October 22, 2012. On October 24 I drove to Brooklyn, New York, to join HEART 9/11 in helping people recover from the storm. We spent our first week or so shoveling mud and sand out of people's basements, including tearing down wet sheetrock and ripping up ruined floors, often leaving nothing but beams and studs in what had once been lovely middle-class homes. Shortly after that, HEART 9/11 decided to focus its efforts on the community of Gerritsen Beach in Brooklyn, New York. Gerritsen had 1,800 homes of which 1,799 had been moderately to severely damaged. All the cars in the community had been totaled by flooding.

In mid-December, John Douglas, President of Gerritsen Beach Cares, decided we couldn't sustain our seven-day-a-week effort so we would start taking Sundays off. Other than that, I was there every day for two months until sometime in December 2012. After December 2012, I was there one evening a week to run resilience training until May 2014.

During that period I applied the BATHE and positive BATHE techniques. Yet, I never learned what it was like for the people of Gerritsen Beach to survive that horrible night and the loss of their homes, cars, and often jobs. What I did learn was what it was like for the hundreds of individuals I had the honor to meet and work with. Everyone's life had been forever changed by the same experience: a storm of historic proportions. No two lives had been changed in the same way. For the person whose partner of many decades had died just a short time before the hurricane, the changes were compounding and prolonging an already painful grieving process. For the single parent who just moved into a home with the kids, a new independent life was threatened. For people with pre-existing medical conditions, homes filled with mold threatened their health in unique and frightening ways long after the hurricane was gone. For the single parent who was an essential worker in the aftermath of the hurricane, it meant a threat to hard-won child custody. For people such as John Douglas, it meant stepping up to lead Gerritsen Beach Cares, which led the recovery efforts at the same time he rebuilt his own home (because of mold and new requirements to raise homes, he had to rebuild three times).

Everyone already had a life of personal challenges and complications before they experienced a disaster or tragedy. No two people are changed in the same way—even people in the same relationship or family.

On December 14, 2012, the horrific Sandy Hook School massacre took place. Shortly thereafter, Bill Keegan, President of HEART 911, and I were asked to attend a conference to bring the Newtown, Connecticut, community together to begin trying to heal and move forward. During the day Bill and I spent several hours with a roomful of first responders. The Newtown and State Police, as well as officers from nearby towns, had responded and were still responding along with firefighters and emergency medical technicians (EMTs). Every one of these brave people was changed forever. Bill and I listened emphatically to all of their painful stories. For the next two years we met with the Newtown police including the Chief, the patrol officers, and the Union officers. Again, we used the BATHE and positive BATHE technique. And we learned yet again: No two people were changed the same way.

On May 20, 2013, an EF-5 tornado (using the Enhanced Fujita Scale) struck Moore, Oklahoma. My great friends Jack and Phyllis Poe had just moved to Moore from Oklahoma City. They had recently retired as Oklahoma City police chaplains. Their idea of retirement was to begin serving the Moore Police Department. As we moved through the debris field trying to secure the few standing homes, we listened to hundreds of people. Because we knew the importance of listening, a member of Local 79[20] of the New York State Laborers Union realized a woman was terrified to stay in her home because the glass patio door was blown out and the front door wouldn't lock. When we had passed through and asked if she needed anything, she had said, "No, I'm fine." Thank God the Union member took the time to really listen. We went back and used parts of torn off roofs to cover the hole left by the patio door and fixed the front door so she could lock it.

Once again, we learned no two people are changed in the same way by the same tragic experience.

Using empathetic techniques won us the trust of the people devastated by tragedies ranging from Hurricane Sandy to Sandy Hook to Moore, Oklahoma. It won their trust because we demonstrated that we really wanted to understand and help them as individuals.

Traditionally, we've often been advised to follow the Golden Rule taken from the Gospel of St. Matthew: "Do unto others as you would have them do unto you" (Matthew 7:12).

The premise of the Golden Rule is that people are fundamentally similar with similar experiences, thoughts, aspirations, and emotions. That premise leads us to the conclusion that people are all like us and, therefore, want to be treated the way we want to be treated. Michael J. Bennett points out that following the Golden Rule keeps us in sympathy with others so that we assume others' reactions and feelings are the same as ours would be—as if we all share the same reality. According to Bennett, the assumption of one reality is the basis for ethnocentricity, which leads to bias and racism. Bennett suggests that "we must assume essential differences among people and allow for multiple realities. When we apply these principles to ourselves, it leads us to the communication strategy of empathy, whereby we imaginatively experience the world from another person's perspective."[21]

Research has shown that being in empathetic relationships creates a broad range of benefits including increases in:

- Feeling calm
- Ethical behavior
- Imagination
- Self-acceptance

- Altruism
- Reciprocity
- Attraction
- Emotional intelligence

All of these benefits will be critically important as we navigate forward.

As we go forward through this phase of massive Uncertainty into the phase of New Beginnings, we can only hope to achieve a more just, healthier, and safer world if we practice empathy to understand ourselves as individuals.

Loving Kindness

Practicing the loving kindness meditation develops our sense of goodwill, kindness, and warmth toward ourselves and others. When we don't have a sense of goodwill, kindness, and warmth toward ourselves, we are blocked from relating positively and productively to others. Similarly, it is difficult to overcome harsh or negative feelings toward someone and build a strong relationship. Loving kindness removes this difficulty.

It has also been found that loving kindness increases the tone or functioning of the vagus nerve, which is the longest nerve in the autonomic nervous system. It regulates heart rate, perspiration, blood pressure, digestion, and speaking.

Loving kindness has also been found to increase the gray matter in areas of the brain responsible for the management of emotions—including anxiety.[22]

Finally, as we strive for racial equality and a more just society, loving kindness meditation has been found to reduce bias against underrepresented minority groups and the homeless.[23]

The Empathic Conversation

Practicing the five behaviors that define an empathic conversation consistently will, as with any behavior, rewire your brain to make these behaviors your default when your brain perceives appropriate signals.

For example, you're sitting in your living room reading the paper on your tablet when your 14-year-old daughter, also reading her tablet, quietly says, "I didn't have such a good day at school." The addictive nature of tablets and iPhones[24] has wired our brains to treat inputs other than those coming from our devices as interruptions. Your brain is wired to unintentionally ignore the potential importance of your daughter's comment. You both return to your tablets.

Now assume you have practiced empathic conversation consistently for 60 days. You now have durable circuits that make being curious and listening intently your automatic responses to signals from other people. Now when your daughter says, "I didn't have such a good day at school," your automatic response is to focus on your daughter—her words, tone, and body language. Your next response is to ask questions that start a conversation and then to continue to listen and observe intently as she shares more.

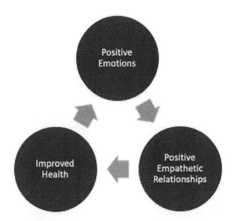

Figure 22: Mutual Reinforcement of Empathetic
Relationships, Health, and Positive Emotions

I want to draw our attention to the fifth behavior—Be yourself: Be comfortable talking about you. That behavior is to be vulnerable. It's being truly open, which requires facing uncertainty, risk, and emotional exposure. It's truly being fully present and engaged with another person.

Brené Brown has done groundbreaking research on the power of being vulnerable.[25] Brown's research reveals the incredible amount of emotional, cognitive, and social energy we constantly expend to keep up a false façade and keep our authentic self hidden away. As her work shows, it is not just others with whom we keep a false front. It is with us as well. A state of constant comparison between ourselves and others, as well as myths, creates an inner shame against which we defend with the denial of keeping up a false reality. Again, this denial applies to ourselves as well as others.

Learning to be vulnerable in important relationships with others who have earned our trust enables us to take risks and achieve our highest potential. Vulnerability is being truly authentic, which builds the courage to, as Brown says, "dare greatly."

Building empathy has tremendous benefits for leaders of large organizations and small business owners. For instance, as Figure 23 shows, empathic relationships with customers significantly increase customer loyalty and profitability.

SEM analysis results.

Note: PWOM: Positive word-of-mouth; RI: repurchase intentions.

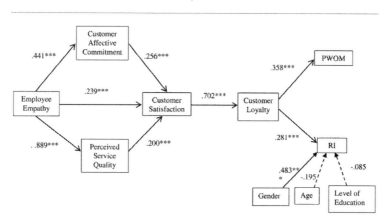

Figure 23: Employee Empathy Drives Customer Loyalty, Positive Word of Mouth, and Repurchase Intentions[26]

This research shows that one of the most powerful ways leaders can drive sustained, profitable growth is to hire and develop sales and service people who are empathetic with customers. As Figure 26 shows, increased employee empathy with customers will increase customers' perception of quality products and services more surely than the majority of improvements to the actual product or service.

In an atmosphere in which everyone is struggling with tremendous uncertainty, empathic human contact between customers/prospects and sales/service people is the only sustainable differentiator. Often we confuse contact with our customers with "relationship" with our customers. For example, many companies use artificial intelligence (AI) to create robotic chat boxes that are clearly not human. Not only does this not build customer relationships, it weakens them. When you invite a customer to chat with your representative, you create an expectation that your representative is a real person. When subpar communication with a robot adds to the customer's frustration, they feel misled so trust is eroded.

Companies that wish to build strong customer relationships may consider replacing robotic chat boxes and phone systems with actual human beings—provided, of course, that the human beings are well trained and are given the authority to serve the customer. Companies may be surprised at the long-term return on investment (ROI) from this investment.

When leaders create empathetic relationships with employees, they gain another set of benefits.

For instance, 81 percent of employees are willing to work longer hours for empathetic leaders. More than 60 percent of employees would work for less compensation if, in return, their leaders were more empathetic. This held true across a range of industry sectors including technology, healthcare, and financial services. Finally, 90 percent of employees are more likely to be retained when they work in an empathetic organization.[27]

The BATHE Technique

The BATHE technique begins by focusing on the situation rather than the person: "What are the things that are going on for you?" By starting this way, it avoids triggering the person's resistance to revealing how they are doing. It bridges the gap between what is happening with the second question: "How do you feel about each of these things?" This maintains a fairly narrow focus, which again avoids triggering resistance and anxiety. The third question—"What troubles you the most?"—shifts to trying to understand the individual's unique experience. The fourth question is framed to create a sense of confidence and agency. It conveys the expectation that the individual can positively improve their experience. The experience of empathy legitimizes how the person experiences and feels about the situation and creates a bond of understanding.

The Positive BATHE Technique

The positive BATHE technique works because it is framed to establish an optimistic point of view. The first question communicates the assumption that even in a very troubling or difficult situation, some good things still happen. It connects good things happening with the experience of positive feelings, which is reinforced by getting the person to reflect on what they are thankful for in this situation. The last question communicates the expectation that the individual can continue to improve how they experience the situation going forward. The expression of empathy provides encouragement and confidence in the person's ability to move forward.

Inclusive Word Choice

The brain is wired to distinguish between groups we belong to and those we don't belong to. When we use words that exclude others (e.g., I, me, my, and myself), we create the perception of a boundary between ourselves and others.

If you work for a new employer and consistently refer to your old employer, you unintentionally create a boundary between you and your new boss and coworkers. Avoid comments such as "When I worked at ABC Company, we did it.... When you use inclusive words and language (e.g., us, we, our, ourselves, and this team), you create boundaries around people, not between them.

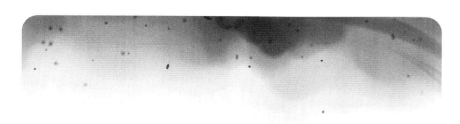

CHAPTER 7

FACT-BASED DECISION-MAKING

Fact-based decision-making is ensuring that conclusions are grounded in facts rather than assumptions or biases. Fact-based decision-making improves the quality of your decisions by minimizing prejudices and expanding the information you consider. Using fact-based decision-making in a group leads to consensus on what the situation is and how to respond to it.

The Routine

There are six behaviors to practice and strengthen fact-based decision-making:

1. The Ladder of Inference
2. Strategic assumptions surfacing and testing
3. Skillful discussion
4. Triangulation
5. Assessing the messenger
6. Pre-mortem
7. The devil's advocate

As with all our chapters, I'll begin with how to build the factor and then say more about why and how it works. That way you can get started building your resilience right away.

The Ladder of Inference

The Ladder of Inference lays out the way we process information to make a decision and take action. The ladder is sitting in a pool of all the information that exists. The first step on the ladder is the information we perceive—the information we select from all that exists. The next step in decision-making is to make assumptions based on the information perceived. Our minds are hard-wired to quickly see patterns in the world. Perceived facts give us a set of puzzle pieces. Assumptions fill in the missing pieces. Assumptions are interpretations of what we see and accept as accurate or certain to take place without proof (i.e., facts that support them).

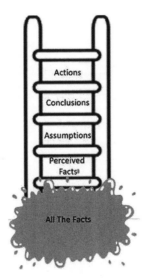

Figure 24: The Ladder of Inference

One way to increase the number of assumptions is to create a stakeholder map or list, which identifies all the people or organizations who are impacted by the problem or solution. The next step on the ladder is to form conclusions. A conclusion is our determination of what the situation is and a decision of how to respond to it. The final step on the ladder is action. Action is what we do to put our decision into effect.

To use the Ladder of Inference to improve your fact-based decision-making:

- Begin anchoring yourself in the pool of "All The Facts."
- `Take your time gathering facts.
- When you have as full a set of perceived facts as possible, allow yourself to add assumptions to fill in the missing pieces of the fact puzzle.
- Next, state or write down your conclusions and the actions you would take based upon them.
- Now force yourself to go to the bottom of the ladder to see if you can pull more facts out of the pool and into the set of facts you perceive.
- Once you have an expanded set of facts, go back up the ladder.
- When you get to your assumptions, compare them with the new facts you have gathered: Do the new facts contradict or support your assumptions?
- At the conclusion level ask yourself: Do the new facts and assumptions change my understanding of the situation and the actions called for?

Tip

- The more you repeat the process of using the Ladder of Inference, the more fact-based your decisions will be.

Strategic Assumptions Surfacing & Testing

The goal of this technique is to sort the assumptions you have generated by using the Ladder of Inference based on their importance to your conclusion (high vs. low) and your level of certainty that they are true (certain vs. uncertain). To begin, draw a matrix (see Figure 25).

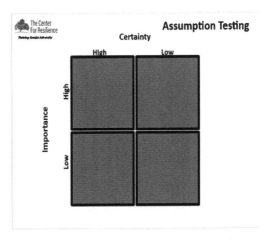

Figure 25: Assumption Testing Grid

Now sort all of your assumptions into the correct box in the matrix. As you go through the process, you may come up with more assumptions. That's great so include them.

Once you have sorted all the assumptions, you have a clear path forward based on the quadrant or box each one is in. As shown in Figure 26, any assumptions in the upper left quadrant—namely, High/High—should be included as the basis for your conclusions. Assumptions in the lower left quadrant—namely, High Certainty/Low Importance—can be included as long as you discount them (i.e., don't treat them as central to your conclusion).

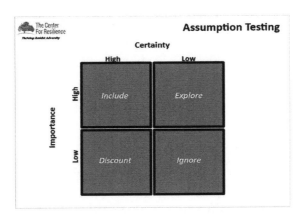

Figure 26: Assumption Testing Grid With Actions

Assumptions in the upper right-hand quadrant—namely, High Importance/Low Certainty—need to be further explored. That is, you need to search for more objective data to increase or decrease the level of certainty that they are true. Finally, any assumptions in the lower right quadrant should be removed from your argument so you won't waste time trying to prove or disprove them.[28]

Skillful Discussion[29]

Skillful discussion uses the Ladder of Inference as the foundation for a group process. The objectives of skillful discussion are to:

- Create a larger set of perceived facts then one person can create
- Develop a shared conclusion and commitment to action

The process is as follows:

- Select an issue to understand or a problem to solve.
- Review the following guidelines with the participants:
  - o Everyone agrees to be open to being influenced with the goal of reaching a shared understanding of the issue/problem.
  - o We will balance advocating our point of view with understanding everyone else's perspectives.
  - o In turn, each person will use the Ladder of Inference to walk the group through their understanding of the issue/problem.
  - o When we don't agree with someone, our first assumption will be that they are aware of perceived facts that we are not. Try the following two responses
    - Can you tell me what facts you are looking at to support that?
    - I hadn't thought of this that way. Can you walk me through it again in more detail?
  - o Don't interrupt.
  - o Avoid judging others and their analysis.

- o   Invoke the Chatham House Rule: Participants can use the information gathered but must not identify the individual or their organization.
- o   We will treat each other with curiosity and respect.
- Optimally, two hours is set aside for a skillful discussion of one significant issue/problem.

To encourage open dialogue and a healthy exchange of ideas, remember the words of Winston Churchill: "If you and I always agree, one of us is redundant."

Triangulation

Triangulation is simply considering data/facts from three different sources when making a decision. For example, in evaluating which college a high school senior should attend, you might consider:

- Information and data provided by the colleges themselves
- National rankings in publications such as *U.S. News & World Report* and/or *The Princeton Review*
- Talking to students from your high school who now attend the colleges you are considering
- Contacting several professors in majors you are interested in to see if they think you are a good fit
- Campus visits or virtual tours

Tips:

- Try to bring in different types of facts. For instance, look at formal evaluations (e.g., *The Princeton Review*), qualitative vs. quantitative information, student feedback, and personal experience (e.g., campus visits or virtual tours).
- Don't rely too much on "big data." Continue to observe people and processes directly. Talk to individuals. "Big data" can be overwhelming and lead you to incorrect conclusions and actions.

Assessing the Messenger

When asking individuals or teams for their advice or recommendations, ask yourself these three questions:

1. How likely is it that the person(s) recommending this decision is(are) acting on self-interest, overconfidence, or their past experiences?
2. Was this person(s) immediately so excited about this idea that they didn't take a careful view at all the facts available?
3. Is this person so influential that others didn't challenge this idea?
4. How credible is this person?

If the answers to one or more of these questions is "Very Likely," then there is probability that the recommendation being put forward is based on significant biases. You should explore these biases before accepting the recommendation.[30]

Pre-Mortem

We often do a post-mortem after a decision has failed. The goal is to answer the question: What went wrong? Before you implement a decision, imagine it was being executed for six months to a year and led to failure. Now ask these questions:

- What went wrong?
- What facts were we unaware of when we committed to this path?

The Devil's Advocate

Ask someone or a group to specifically find facts and assumptions that go against the decision you are considering. Don't argue; just listen.

Why and How It Works!

As Figure 30 illustrates, there are literally hundreds of known cognitive biases or heuristics. Each one of these is a neurologic shortcut in which the goal is to speed up our reaction time. The problem is—to borrow from *Law & Order* scripts—they "assume facts not in evidence." Biases sacrifice accuracy (facts) for efficiency and speed.

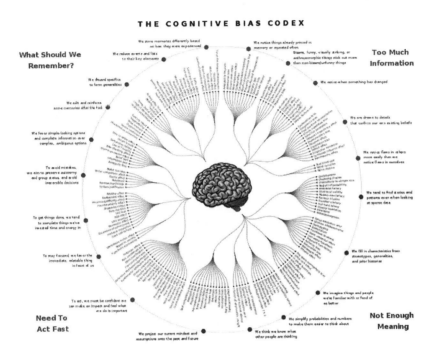

THE COGNITIVE BIAS CODEX

Figure 27: Categorization of 200 Cognitive Biases[31]

When biases are strong, we are likely to jump straight to a conclusion when making a decision before we fully examine the data and information available to us. The more experience you have, the more biases that are wired in your brain, which increases the risk that you will not perceive facts that run counter to the bias.

Unchecked, the wiring of these biases can be so fast that you end up at the top of the ladder after noticing as little as one or two facts. Let's review just five of the most common biases.

Confirmation bias leads us to overweigh information that agrees with our beliefs (not the facts we perceive). Let's imagine that you believe that there must be a treatment for COVID-19 that is highly effective and can be used for everyone infected. You will unintentionally find information through social media, blogs, and talk shows that support your belief. You will also unintentionally avoid or ignore information that successful treatments have not been found. Your confirmation wiring is sizzling. Everything you hear from them makes you sure that you are right.

Now imagine tomorrow a series of studies are released by major medical journals. Each study presents objective evidence that no treatment has been found that can be used with the majority of those infected. The studies are widely reported in the news.

It doesn't matter. The neural circuits creating your confirmation bias are strong and fast. You have cognitively and emotionally shut off considering any new facts that don't agree with your bias.

Availability bias leads us to make decisions based on the information that most easily comes to mind. For example, one of my key clients for several years was the Chairman/CEO of a major grocery store chain in the Northeastern United States. Greg was an extremely passionate leader and merchant. He and I spent a lot of time visiting his stores and speaking with associates and customers. More importantly, my team and I had used data to create a predictive algorithm that defined the customer experience that would drive sustained, profitable growth. Greg endorsed the effort to activate this customer experience across all of the company's grocery stores.

Then Greg took a family vacation to Florida. Well, actually, his wife and sons took a vacation. Greg spent two to three hours each morning managing the company remotely. Then he spent two to three hours visiting grocery stores in Florida. Somehow he still managed to get in a few rounds of golf and spend some time with his family at the pool.

At one well-known Southern grocery chain, Greg was struck by two things. First, every cashier addressed every customer by name. When a customer entered their frequent shopper number, their name came up on the register's screen. Customers reciprocated by calling the cashier's by name after looking at their name tag. It was all very friendly.

The second thing that struck Greg was the carry-out service that associates provided while refusing to accept tips.

The morning Greg returned from Florida, he and I met for breakfast.

"Leo, I had the most amazing experience! We're going to have all our cashiers address each customer by name and offer every customer carry-out service with no tipping allowed."

"Greg, I know where you had that experience. I've seen it myself."

"Then you know firsthand how powerful it is! We have to do it now."

"Greg, that would be a mistake. You've invested a lot of time and money to define and then implement a unique customer experience based on the data from your customers, not customers in Florida."

"So what! I live in the Northeast and loved it. I want a plan from you on how we're going to incorporate this into our customer experience."

"Greg, respectfully, I know that's the wrong decision."

"Leo, I have tremendous respect for you and your team. It would be a shame to part ways because you won't do as I ask."

Five days later, Greg approved the plan to add two additional behaviors to his customer experience: greeting people by name and no-tip carry-out service. To his credit, that afternoon we jumped on the corporate jet and spent the next 48 hours visiting his stores. At each store he would go up to customers and say, "Hi! I'm Greg, and I'm CEO of this company. If our cashiers called you by name as you checked out and other associates carried out your groceries with no tipping, wouldn't that make a better experience for you?"

Nine out of ten customers agreed with Greg. If you look at the way he posed the question, that is exactly what you would expect.

Within one week of implementing the new behaviors, we were observing chaos across the company's stores. Cashiers were reading customers' names off of their credit cards or checks (we didn't have the technology to have the names show up on the register's screen). Examining checks and credit cards made customers uncomfortable and suspicious. When greeted by name, customers responded with reactions such as "How do you know my name?" and "Why are you taking so much time?" and "Are you trying to memorize my credit card number!" Carry-out service was an even bigger disaster. In the case of the

Florida chain, the majority of customers were over 60 years of age and retired. They weren't offended by being offered carry-out service. They appreciated it.

Greg's customer demographics were far different. His stores attracted working- and middle-class families. The majority were between the ages of 27 and 52 years old. Those at the higher end of that range were insulted that some "kid" thought they couldn't handle their own groceries. Those at the lower end of the age range greeted the offer of no-tip carry-out service with tremendous suspicion.

Within three weeks, Greg reversed his decision—a decision he had made based on the data most readily available to his thought process. His data were collected in a very different context than his company operated in, namely, Florida vs. the Northeast. His data were collected in his stores when he introduced himself as the CEO, which caused people to give him the answer they thought he wanted to hear.

Recency bias leads us to come to conclusions and make decisions based on the most recent information we receive. For example, imagine you own a bar and restaurant. Prior to the pandemic and the shutdown, one of your servers, Stan, had been consistently showing up late for his shift, getting guest orders wrong, and being rude to several guests. In fact, just before the shutdown, you had carefully reviewed his performance and provided coaching and warnings. You decided you have no choice but to fire him. The next day you were forced to shut down your bar and restaurant.

On the day you were allowed to open for outdoor dining, Stan showed up early and helped with all the changes that had to be made before you could start serving guests. When you did open up, Stan was very cheerful in serving guests, careful in taking their orders, and genuinely apologetic when an order was delayed. The recency bias kicked in so you decide you had misjudged Stan. It was probably because you were so stressed before the shutdown.

A week later eight guests sitting at four different tables left without paying their bill because Stan had yelled at one couple: "You're the most unreasonable people I've ever met. You're totally out of it. Why don't you go somewhere else?"

At a critical time the recency bias caused you to misjudge Stan at great cost to you and your business.

Sunk cost bias is when you continue to spend money, time, or effort on something that clearly isn't working—simply because you have already invested in it.

Here's a simple example. You hear about a new book being released. It sounds very interesting. You decide to treat yourself and pay $29 for a hardcover version so you don't have to wait for it to come out in paperback or digital. After dinner you sit down with the book and a glass of iced tea, ready to enjoy reading for two or three hours before going to bed. After 45 minutes it's clear you aren't enjoying reading the book at all. It is simply BORING! Yet you keep reading because you don't want to lose the 45 minutes you have already sunk into reading this boring book. So you keep at it. Actually, you go to bed half-an-hour late because you kept reading just to get past the boring part.

Let's go back to running your bar and restaurant. You decide that you are going to offer appetizers and entrees at 50 percent off—well below your cost to make and serve them. Your thinking is that people will buy enough high-margin drinks to make the deal profitable.

After a week you review your revenues and profits. It's not working. On average, each patron is having 1.5 drinks. Your break-even point is three drinks. You also recall noticing that most people are leaving as soon as they finish eating. As you are operating at 75 percent capacity, your service is really fast. The simple fact is guests aren't in your establishment long enough to have two, much less three, drinks. You also notice that people are choosing house liquors, wines, and beers. Very few people are spending money on their favorite scotch, burgundy, or ale. The evidence is quite clear that your strategy isn't working, but you can't afford to lose what you have already spent on the promotion. So you keep it going, deepening your financial losses with every hour you are open.

The bandwagon effect is when we adopt the opinions or behaviors we see most people taking. Psychologist Solomon Asch conducted a classic experiment to see how this worked. He had a group of people line up. The first seven people were confederates, aware of the experiment and the role they were to play. The eighth person was the experimental subject, a real participant. Asch showed the group a line he called the target or standard and a set of four more lines. He asked the group which of the four lines was the same length as the standard.

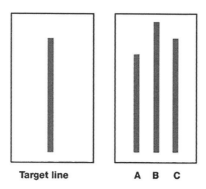

Target line   **A   B   C**

Figure 28: Replication of Experimental Lines Used by Asch

In half the trials, the confederates each said that the correct answer was line A, which was clearly shorter than the target line. In the other half of the trials, all the confederates said B was the correct answer; line B was clearly longer than the target line. Approximately 75 precent of the participants answered A or B rather than the obvious correct answer C. In other words, they went along with the crowd or "jumped on the bandwagon."

Again, these are just five of the hundreds of biases that our experience has hard-wired into our brains. The paradox is that the more experience we have, the more our decisions are driven by these biases and the less we make decisions based on facts.

Each of the seven behaviors that develop fact-based decision-making challenge the existing neural structures that create and activate the biases. In addition, if you consistently practice these behaviors, you will build new neural networks that will override your biases and enable you to gather and consider a full set of facts as the foundation for your conclusions and actions.

Here's a safety tip. You are headed for trouble as soon as you think or say things such as:

- "I've been in this industry my whole career. Nobody knows it better than I do."
- "I've seen this before; I know exactly what to do."
- "We tried this before, and it didn't work."

The world is changing at an unprecedented pace on all fronts. We rely on our previous experience while minimizing the collection of current facts at our peril.

Here's why each of the techniques works.

The Ladder of Inference

The steps on the Ladder of Inference are like a workout routine. The exercise is to go up one step at a time and come down one step at a time. As a workout routine builds muscle, the Ladder of Inference builds neural networks. It also signals when you are veering away from the process of building your thought process on facts. For example, when I'm coaching senior executives, they will often bring up a decision they have made and are about to act on. When I politely walk them down the ladder and ask what facts they used to make their decision, they are often taken aback when they realize they can't name any facts they considered in arriving at their decision. That's a sure sign of cognitive biases at work. These are highly experienced and successful people. The more experience, the stronger their biases. Once they've experienced this, they usually are very open to adopting the Ladder of Inference as one technique to improve their decision-making.

An example of how fast people can jump from one fact to actions comes from a friend of mine who is a highly successful executive and African American. Almost 50 years ago, he attended the University of Notre Dame. He tells me that when people ask him where he went to school and he responds, "Notre Dame," 95 percent of the time the next question is "What sport did you play?" My friend has exceptionally high emotional intelligence and usually responds: "None. I was just a student."

The implication of "What sport did you play?" is that an African American couldn't be admitted to a top university such as Notre Dame without an athletic scholarship. Such a question is most often produced by a bias that African Americans aren't smart or academically prepared. The way my friend handles this racist thinking makes some people aware of what they asked implied and how insulting it is.

If we are going to really achieve racial equality, all of us are going to have to learn to discover our racial and social biases. We need to use fact-based decision-making to eliminate them so we can think and act more justly.

I'm embarrassed to say I have my own biases based on my experience. My wife and I have been actively working with the homeless for many years. One day I was attending a meeting of my Men's Ministry. We were talking about running a clothing drive for one of the men's shelters. One of our members said: "We can never underestimate the importance of this work. You never know how life-changing it can be....I lived in that shelter for almost three years. It's how I got to where I am today." Today he has a very successful contracting business, a great marriage, four children, and is highly respected in the community. He's also white.

What he shared totally challenged a number of biases I had—some of which I didn't realize I had. He made me look at facts at the bottom of the Ladder of Inference that caused my biases to crumble—fortunately.

None of us are immune to biases, and moving forward requires us to challenge and correct them.

Strategic Assumptions Surfacing and Testing

Why this works is very similar to the Ladder of Inference: It provides a step-by-step process for evaluating our assumptions. Following the process rewires the brain. Again, it reduces the impact of our biases. It creates a neural network that forces us not just to identify our assumptions but to really assess them. When we categorize some assumptions as High Importance/Low Certainty, it drives us back to the bottom of the Ladder of Inference to search for facts that increase or decrease the level of certainty. The neural circuits that are created become mutually reinforcing.

Skillful Discussion

Many times when we think we're having a group discussion, we're simply not! Often we are arguing about our conclusions and decisions, not discussing them. The assumption is that one of us is right and the rest of us are wrong. We resort to power plays rather than listening to one another. Often the person who shouts the loudest and the longest wins by exhausting everyone else.

Some people simply decide not to participate and remain silent as they watch the fray.

Some folks don't speak the truth. Instead of honestly sharing how they view the situation, they nod in agreement with the person they think will "win" the argument. The result is bad decisions are made, the wrong actions are taken, and relationships are not built.

When you adopt skillful discussion, you shift from win/lose to finding the best possible solution. You move from conflict to inquiry. You build trust, not animosity.

The simple process of asking each person to walk up or down the Ladder of Inference creates relationships of mutual respect, trust, and collaboration.

Collectively, you build a much more complete set of facts to consider, giving your group process of moving up the ladder to conclusions and actions a much stronger foundation. Over time, as skillful discussion becomes hard-wired in many peoples' brains, you will shift the entire culture of your entire business, organization, or community into a culture that will be able to make powerful changes to move forward.

Triangulation

As we discussed earlier, many cognitive biases lead us to overweigh or under weigh sources of information. We draw conclusions and take actions based on a biased perspective rather than a set of reliable facts.

Let's say you have a fishing boat. You're out fishing and hit an amazing school of fish. You're bringing in fish nonstop for two hours. You stop fishing, not because the fish stopped biting but because you are just exhausted. You definitely want to find this exact spot again.

You look at your compass and set the bearing to return to your dock, which gives you a straight line. Next time you're out you can reverse the heading/course and set out to this new "favorite spot." But where do you stop? On a straight line you can keep going until you pass over the spot and head out to sea. The answer is to take two more compass bearings before you weigh anchor. There is only one spot on the globe where three compass bearings will intersect.

We use the same logic in using triangulation to make fact-based decisions. You ground yourself in at least three different sources of information. The idea is that if three independent, trusted sources give the same facts and conclusions, you can have high confidence in relying on them.

For example, in the midst of the pandemic perhaps you are unsure about whether or not wearing masks is truly an effective way of reducing the spread of COVID-19 and protecting yourself and others. If you watch the news media, you'll likely come away confused and anxious. If you consult the websites of major medical centers, they will often cite the same studies—for instance, those conducted by the CDC. This doesn't mean their advice is wrong; it just means it isn't independent. In addition to reading the CDC's recommendations, I did a Google Scholar search and read several independent studies—all of which concluded that wearing masks is not only a good idea but is essential.[32] So three independent sources give me total confidence that wearing a mask is essential to my health and the health of those around me.

Assessing the Messenger

As teenagers, we learned "always consider the source." The reason this works is very simple. Asking yourself three simple questions about anyone giving you advice or recommendations forces you to think about them objectively. Eventually, this becomes hard-wired and controls for a wide range of cognitive biases.

Pre-Mortem

Assuming the failure of a decision forces us to add new assumptions to our thinking and, in turn, to search for more facts. Taking the perspective that we failed forces us to find facts that explain that failure—even before we begin acting on our decision. It strengthens the neural networks that hard-wire the use of the Ladder of Inference.

The Devil's Advocate

Again, here's another simple and powerful technique. Assigning someone to attack your logic ensures the facts and assumptions that contradict your thinking are brought into consideration. The devil's advocate doesn't have to be brave enough to share contrary facts; it's their job! This technique is especially powerful in fighting the bandwagon effect and groupthink.

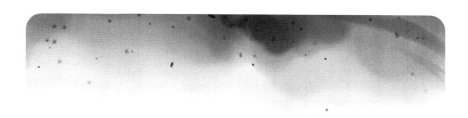

CHAPTER 8

AGILITY

Agility is the ability to quickly change course to achieve an objective in the face of challenges and obstacles. If you've read Chapter 4 on Pragmatic Optimism: The First Factor to Concentrate On, you'll recall the five things we cannot change—one of which is "things don't go according to plan." Building your agility is an important way to plan for that reality.

The Agility Routine

There are four behaviors to practice consistently to build your agility:

1. Framing-reframing
2. Brain writing
3. Triggered brain walking
4. Wishing diamonds
5. Aligning options

As with all our chapters, I'll begin with how to build the factor and then say more about why and how it works. That way you can get started building your resilience right away.

Framing-Reframing

Reframing is the process of creating new frames through which to understand and respond to a challenge or situation.

- Simply approach any challenge/situation in which you are having difficulty finding a solution by asking a series of "what if..." questions:
    - o What if I had unlimited time/money/help to solve this?
    - o What if I were an engineer/doctor/comedian/ lawyer, how would I solve this?
    - o What if I had solved this same problem in the past, how did I do it?
    - o What if I failed to solve this problem in the past, what would I do differently this time?
    - o What if I absolutely had to take one step forward now, what would it be?
- The questions often appear absurd.
    - o They should.
- It's that radical shift in your viewpoint that enables you to see the problem/challenge from a fresh perspective.

Brain Writing

Brain writing is a group agility technique.

- Identify a challenge facing the group.
- Give each person a pen/pencil and a piece of paper.
- Have each person write the challenge at the top of their paper.
- Have each person write down an idea for overcoming the challenge.
- Have everyone pass their sheet of paper to the person on their left.
- Repeat the passing until each sheet of paper has been passed around the group four or five times.

- Pass the papers around one more time with each person circling the best idea on each sheet of paper.
- Then use the list of circled ideas to fill in the options column on the Aligning Options Grid (see Figure 30).

Triggered Brain Walking

Triggered brain walking is another group agility technique. Usually you do this technique inside a large room; if you want to do it outside, simply use flipcharts and easels to post the ideation stations.

- Identify the challenge you need to overcome.
- Set up 10 to 12 ideation stations.
  - o Each station consists of:
    - Several sheets of flipchart paper
    - Three or four markers of different colors
    - An image of a "trigger"
    - For instance, if your challenge is how to increase take-out orders from your restaurant, triggers might be the logos of well-known companies.
- Bring your group together and tell everyone the challenge you are facing.
- Depending on the size of the group, have one to three people stand in front of each ideation station.
- Tell the group to write down potential solutions to the challenge that are "triggered" by the picture or image above the flipchart paper.
- Every three minutes have the participants "walk their brain" clockwise to the next ideation station.
- After five or six times around the ideation stations, have the participants make one more pass and circle the best idea at each station.
- Then use the list of circled ideas to fill in the options column on the Aligning Options Grid (see Figure 30).

Wishing Diamonds

- Begin by drawing a diagram (see Figure 29).
- Write in the challenge you want to address.
- Now, for the moment, assume that anything is possible.
- In the top diamond start writing in what you wish was possible to solve this challenge.
  - o Remember anything is possible.
- After you've written down as many wishes as you like, pick one.
- In the second diamond write down ways you could come close to realizing your wish.
- After you have written down a number of ideas that get you as close as possible to your wish, pick one.
- Now in the third diamond write down the pluses and minuses of the idea.
  - o The pluses are simply written down.

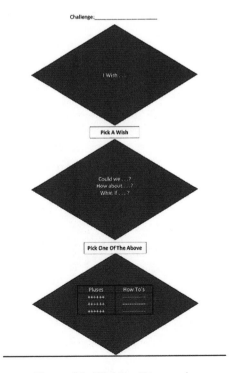

Figure 29: Wishing Diamonds

- o The minuses are written down as questions (i.e., "How do we overcome...?"or "How do we get around...?"
- o If the pluses outnumber or outweigh the minuses that you can't eliminate or solve for, then begin to implement your idea.
- o If the minuses that can't be eliminated or solved outweigh your pluses, go back up to the first item at the top, pick another wish, and restart the process.

Aligning Options

Before tackling any problem, you can develop three or more potential solutions. When the first solution is blocked, you quickly shift to executing the next solution.

To structure this process, you can use this worksheet (see Figure 30).

	Option Evaluation Grid				
	Objective:				
Criteria / Options	Criteria 1	Criteria 2	Criteria 3	Criteria 4	Criteria 5
	Fulfills / Does not fulfill	Fulfills / Does not fulfill	Fulfills / Does not fulfill	Fulfills / Does not fulfill	Fulfills / Does not fulfill
	Fulfills / Does not fulfill	Fulfills / Does not fulfill	Fulfills / Does not fulfill	Fulfills / Does not fulfill	Fulfills / Does not fulfill
	Fulfills / Does not fulfill	Fulfills / Does not fulfill	Fulfills / Does not fulfill	Fulfills / Does not fulfill	Fulfills / Does not fulfill
	Fulfills / Does not fulfill	Fulfills / Does not fulfill	Fulfills / Does not fulfill	Fulfills / Does not fulfill	Fulfills / Does not fulfill
	Fulfills / Does not fulfill	Fulfills / Does not fulfill	Fulfills / Does not fulfill	Fulfills / Does not fulfill	Fulfills / Does not fulfill

Figure 30: Aligning Options Worksheet

1. State your objective.
   - In the second row at the top of the worksheet, write down your objective as clearly and specifically as possible.
   - For example: Pick a family vacation that everyone looks forward to and enjoys.
2. Determine your criteria.
   - Across the top you will see boxes labeled Criteria 1 through Criteria 5.
   - You can have as many as eight criteria.
   - In each of these boxes write in one specific criteria.
   - In our family vacation example, some criteria could be:
     - Within our budget
     - Water sports available
     - Not a huge resort
     - Not more than a three-hour flight
     - Nature hiking/touring available
3. Brainstorm your options.
   - The first column on the left is labeled Options
   - Without considering your criteria, brainstorm as many options as you can.
4. Evaluate your options against your criteria.
   - Once you have at least eight options, evaluate each one against all of your criteria.
5. Select your two or three best options.
6. Choose one of the options to pursue first.
   - Keep the other one or two options in reserve.
7. When the first option doesn't work, go immediately to the second option.

Tips

- Be as specific as you can when writing your objective.
- Once you have decided on the criteria against which to evaluate your options, don't change them.

- Evaluate all the options against all the criteria.
  - o Don't stop evaluating an option as soon as it doesn't meet a criteria.
- Commit to going with the second option if the first doesn't work and going with the third option if the second doesn't work.
- Notice, after evaluating your options, there is almost never a perfect solution.
  - o This frees you emotionally to move forward with "less than perfect."

Why and How It Works!

Researchers have found that people who are resilient see setbacks and failures as things that can and will happen to anyone.[33] Again, see the discussion about the five things we cannot change in Chapter Two on Pragmatic Optimism: The First Factor to Concentrate On. They act on the acceptance of these situations by creating a range of options to respond to setbacks or solve challenges. For major issues, they imagine a range of possible scenarios ranging from fantastic to neutral to total failure. Again, they create options to respond to each of these potential scenarios. The result is whatever situation evolves, they are able to respond.

Even if the situation that evolves is not precisely one they had planned for, the discipline of planning and the inventory of options considered give them the ability to respond confidently, quickly, and effectively.

The two sets of behaviors—framing-reframing and aligning options—provide processes that, if practiced consistently for ~70 days, will rewire your brain to think and act with greater agility.

Framing-Reframing

As mentioned earlier, our approach to developing resilience is grounded in the body of neuroscience that shows that the brain is constantly growing and changing (i.e., it is plastic). Any consistent experience will create, or wire, strong neural networks—networks that will fire first in response to any stimuli that appears to be related to those networks.

Experience is a double-edged sword. The more experience you have in a particular area, the faster your brain will see even partial information as a signal to address the current circumstance based on what you have done in the past. In other words, your brain becomes wired to use a frame of reference created by your past experiences and what worked and didn't work. Your brain is wired to see new situations as similar to old ones. Plus, your brain will distort perceptions of a current challenge to fit to old problems/challenges.

Let's say you are in charge of construction and facilities for a large medical center. You know the building and health codes like the back of your hand. In renovating one of the oldest buildings in the medical center, you discover old fireplaces and chimneys are hidden behind the walls put up from multiple renovations. Your brain sees a fireplace and immediately fires off: fireplace = code violations = delays + ripping out the fireplaces = cost overruns.

Overwhelmed, you call the COO and ask him to meet you on one of the renovation floors. When the COO arrives, he can't see a solution that avoids delays and massive cost overruns. Fireplaces in patient rooms are against code.

Then the COO practices framing/reframing by asking the question: "If I were in a business in which having working fireplaces in every room was an advantage, what business would I be in?" After about 30 minutes of brainstorming with you (the construction manager) and a few other team members, the answer "luxury hotels" is offered. After a little more discussion the team becomes enthusiastic over the idea of creating a luxury inpatient unit for very affluent patients and their families.

Then the team gets stuck in the old "frame" again. Fireplaces are against code. We can't do this.

The COO reframes again: "What makes a fireplace a fireplace?" Answer: The ability to build a fire. Immediately you realize if you seal the chimney damper of each fireplace, you won't be able to build a fire in the "fireplace."

Sound like a fanciful tale? It's a true story. It took place in a New York City hospital in the early 1980s. The luxury inpatient units brought in $1,000 in premiums each night. With 50 units that amounted to $14 million in extra revenues per year—paid by the affluent individuals, not their insurance companies. Plus, the affluent individuals were so impressed with the luxury and care they received that many of them contributed to the medical center's development fund, which amounted to many millions more.

Framing/reframing forces your brain to ignore the wiring based on experience and to use new networks that respond to a new framing of the reality you face.

> *Please note: The next three techniques—brain writing, triggered brain walking, and wishing diamonds—I learned from my dear friend and colleague Bryan W. Mattimore, Chief Idea Guy, The Growth Engine. Bryan is a true genius at agility and innovation. A number of years ago I was helping a global bank start their innovation group Strategic Growth Initiatives. I was lucky and smart enough to ask Bryan to join our team. He led us by using his techniques, which resulted in our identifying $2.9 billion in potential new businesses. Along the way we learned a tremendous amount and had great fun. I strongly recommend you read both of Bryan's books: 99% INSPIRATION: A Real World Guide to Business Creativity and IDEA STORMERS: How to Lead and Inspire Creative breakthroughs. You can reach Bryan at bmattimore@growth-engine.com and visit his website at https://growth-engine.com/.*

Brain Writing[34]

Brain writing is like brainstorming propelled by high-octane jet fuel. In brainstorming folks have to wait their turn to contribute an idea. Ideas are forgotten. People lose interest. People decide not to offer ideas because they are introverted, or they are afraid the group won't see their idea as "good enough." Relatively speaking, the number of ideas generated by brainstorming is modest.

Passing sheets around for people to jot down new ideas generates a creativity velocity that short-circuits all those cognitive biases and inhibitions. When it comes to being agile, having a large inventory of ideas/potential solutions is critical.

Triggered Brain Walking

When Bryan Mattimore designed this technique, we were working with a global bank. The triggers he selected for the ideation stations were logos of iconic companies—BUT NOT other banks or financial institutions. He used Amazon, Apple, Facebook, FedEx, Google, IBM, Marriott, McDonald's, MicroSoft, Ritz Hotels, Southwest Air, and UPS, among others. We usually had 80 to 100 participants. So we often had 30 ideation stations arranged around a very large conference room.

The triggers effectively caused everyone to reframe the challenge we were trying to solve. As they rotated around the room, they looked at each trigger and were asked: "If you were (e.g., Amazon, McDonalds), how would you solve this challenge?"

Responding in front of dozens of colleagues created a feeling of competition. That competitiveness, combined with the speed of the process, overcame a tremendous number of cognitive biases and yielded some really fantastic and actionable ideas.

Plus, this uses "outside-in" thinking. How would I answer this if I were in the fast-food business, the online sales business, the advertising business?

Wishing Diamonds

Just yesterday the Arthur Avenue business community announced that as New York City enters phase two of reopening as part of the COVID-19 reopening plan, they will convert their community to resemble an Italian piazza. Arthur Avenue in The Bronx, New York, is a predominantly Italian business community of wonderful bakeries, butchers, produce markets, delis, and restaurants—many 100 years old. Pre-pandemic, you could barely drive through the streets or walk along the sidewalks because of the large crowds. One shop only makes fresh pasta. To get your order filled on a Saturday, you used to have to be in line by 7 a.m. and be prepared to wait. Restaurants enjoyed long lines of diners and didn't offer carry-out. Arthur Avenue is the epitome of a small business community.

The shutdown hit them terribly hard.

To move forward, they came together as a community and decided to create a replica of an Italian piazza—an idea reflecting much of the community's roots in honoring a people and nation that is well on the way to recovery after one the world's most severe shutdowns and a solution that encourages people taking precautions (i.e., social distancing, mask wearing, and handwashing).

Aligning Options

Your boss walks up to you and says: "I have this problem....I need a solution in 30 minutes. Come to my office with the solution."

You have 30 minutes to solve a challenging problem. What are you most likely to do in response to this challenge? Start to think about solutions; you haven't got much time!

You come up with your first idea. You quickly start to evaluate it. It's flawed! Can't bring that to the boss. With only 26 minutes to go you come up with your second, third, fourth, and fifth ideas—all have a flaw. Time is running out, and the ideas are beginning to take longer and longer. Emotionally, you have filled a mental garbage can full of flawed ideas. The next idea has to be the "one"!

You have an idea so all your emotional and cognitive biases kick in. You see what you want and need to see. With one minute to go, you run to your boss's office.

You pitch it. He throws up on it! You argue that it's a great idea (you have no alternative). Your amygdala is firing like crazy; you can't flee so you have to fight for your idea. This does not end well. Curtain closes, end of scene.

Now let's rewrite that scene using the aligning options tool.

Your boss walks up to you and says: "I have this problem...I need a solution in 30 minutes. Come to my office with the solution."

You have 30 minutes to solve a challenging problem. You open up your laptop and pull up the aligning options tool.

The criteria against which to evaluate all solutions/plans are already partially completed. The first four criteria are the four pillars of the company strategy. In that top row you fill in the "Objective" your boss has just given you. You fill in two more criteria against which to evaluate your options. The criteria are based on your boss's goals for his team for the year.

Now, without even looking at the criteria, you fill the first column with 10 or maybe more options to solve the problem the boss gave you. When you're done only 10 minutes have passed, and you have 11 potential solutions to the problem the boss gave you.

You're feeling good. You have time and plenty of options to work with. Now you evaluate each option against all of the criteria. You're using the Excel version so scoring against criteria is a matter of simply clicking on dropdown menus. The scores for each idea get automatically tallied by the spreadsheet.

When you're finished you haven't got one perfect idea. You're reminded that means you're doing a good, thorough, and objective job because in the real world there are no perfect solutions.

You have got three pretty good ideas—each one with somewhat different scores against the criteria. With five minutes to go you do a three-minute breathing meditation (see page 37) to clear your head and ground yourself. With two minutes left you calmly walk down to your boss's office. Putting your hand up to knock, you practice arriving mindfully (see page 38). He says: "Come in."

You present the idea you think is best—and how it scores against the criteria. It scores low against the criteria of "Simplifies Customer Experience." That's okay because you have three pretty good ideas. One of the other two ideas scores a perfect "5" on "Simplifies Customer Experience."

You don't argue desperately with your boss. You show him an alternative solution based on his feedback. He likes it and tells you to go with it.

You suggest that since nothing ever goes according to plan (see the five things we cannot change discussion on page 26), you would like his permission to immediately pivot to the second option and then the third option as each one hits an inevitable road block. That will keep the momentum going. Of course, you'll inform your boss each time you pivot.

He agrees.

You won. You leave, having increased your boss's opinion of you. You're more confident, which is just the way you want to feel as you begin to execute a new plan.

Summary

As we discussed in Chapter 1, we have left the phase of Endings and are now deeply immersed in the phase of Uncertainty, struggling to reach the phase of New Beginnings.

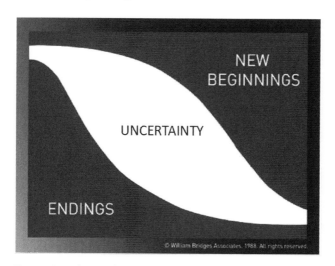

Figure 31: The Bridges Model of Transformation Adapted
Adapted from William Bridges Associates.

As we go forward in this journey, agility will be critical to our success in terms of emotional, economic, health, and social factors. As I write on Dec. 20, 2020, the United States has reached a new high of 50,000 people per day newly infected with COVID-19. For the moment we have failed to stem the tide of the disease. To do so, we need to be agile in how we respond to the challenge of safeguarding our health, our lives, and our economy. As in all disasters, circumstances and challenges change significantly every 12 hours.

We're like a ship sailing through Uncertainty after a terrible storm has devastated our home port. There is no dock, no harbor, and no port to which we can return. We have to continue to sail forward, agilely, rapidly changing course as necessary until we reach New Beginnings when our agility will be further tested as we create a new healthier, safer, and more just world.

If agility is so critical to our success, then why is it not discussed until Chapter 8? The reason is very simple. Before we can practice agility or fact-based decision-making, we must quell our anxiety by building pragmatic optimism, focus, and empathy. We can't be agile if paralyzed by anxiety and fear.

We have to learn to defeat our cognitive biases and engage in fact-based decision-making before we address being agile. Agility is grounded in the ability to think calmly while discerning the changing facts around us.

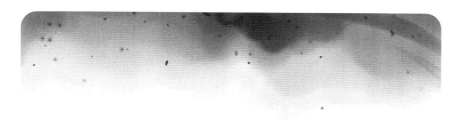

CHAPTER 9

BALANCED GOAL-SETTING

B alanced goal-setting is the pursuit of meaningful and measurable goals in five life arenas: work, family, health, spirituality, and community.

The Routine

There are two behaviors to practice consistently to build your balanced goal-setting:

1. The four most powerful questions
2. The four most powerful questions tool

As with all our chapters, I'll begin with how to build the factor and then say more about why and how it works. That way you can get started building your resilience right away.

The Four Most Powerful Questions

The four most powerful questions are a set of questions that are the surest way to create a mindset that can motivate yourself or others.

The questions are:

- What do you want?

- What are you doing?
- How is that working?
- What is your plan?

When trying to create change in yourself or others, simply ask these four questions. It's that simple. The questions reveal disconnects between what you want and what you are doing.

More discussion about how this simple and powerful technique works is provided in this chapter's section on why and how it works.

The Four Most Powerful Questions Tool

The tool walks you through a process of asking the four most powerful questions in terms of what you want and are doing with regard to family, health, spirituality, community, and profession.

Figure 32 provides a worksheet for the four most powerful questions tool.

	FAMILY	HEALTH	SPIRITUALITY	COMMUNITY	PROFESSIONALLY
What do I want? (in each of these four life areas) Advice: Be as specific as possible. For instance, professionally "A Challenging Job" is not as clear as "A Job That Challenges My Ability To Innovate In (Area of Expertise)."					
What am I doing? (to achieve what I want) Advice: Again being specific is key. For example under Health/Spirit "get in better shape" is not as clear as "Be able to run a 5k"					

	FAMILY	HEALTH	SPIRITUALITY	COMMUNITY	PROFESSIONALLY
How is that working? (Is what I am doing getting me closer to my objective?) **Advice** Be as objective and specific as possible.					
What is my plan? (to achieve my objective) **Advice** Be honest. If you don't have a plan or don't know what to do – the other tools and techniques in our resilience learning will help.					

Figure 32: Worksheet From the Four Most Powerful Questions Tool

Completing this worksheet deserves thought and time to help you direct your energies, talents, and time toward the things you really value in life.

Tips

- When asking the four most powerful questions, don't press for answers or logic!
    - Many people don't know what they want so answering the four most powerful questions is very hard.
- Don't be frustrated when someone tells you what they are doing is not working and their plan is to keep doing the same thing.
    - Resistance is a natural first response so don't fight it.
    - The four most powerful questions set up a continuous "voice" in a person's head: "What I'm doing isn't working, and I'm going to keep doing it."
    - Eventually, the emotional tension created by that voice makes the person decide to change.

Why and How It Works!
The Four Most Powerful Questions

The four most powerful questions is the strongest technique in getting people to want to change. Let's look at two definitions of motivation:

1. The reason or reasons one has for acting or behaving in a particular way
2. The general desire or willingness of someone to do something

The first definition includes negative reinforcements and punishments in understanding why a person acts or behaves in a certain way. To me, this is not true motivation.

True motivation is about a person having an emotional and/or cognitive desire to do something positive, which is consistent with the second definition. When I use the term motivation or motivating, it is that second definition I'm applying.

The truth is that no one can motivate another person. Yes, you can take away privileges from a child. If they value those privileges enough, they may do what you want, which is simply compliance. They probably won't do it based on an internal drive to do so. Also, children are smart. Take away their iPhone, and they will at least pretend to not miss it, making you feel like you've been an ineffective parent.

The same applies with employees. You can hire, promote, train, pay, suspend, and fire. Again, you may get them to do something, but you won't be creating an internal drive.

Employee engagement was first defined and studied in 1990.[35] In the past 30 years, despite hundreds of millions of dollars spent by corporations and billions of dollars in business losses in the United States alone, we have made little, if any, progress in improving the engagement—or motivation—of employees. Gallup's latest State of the American Workforce[36] reports that in the average US company only 33 percent of employees are engaged, 51 percent are not engaged, and 16 percent are actively disengaged (i.e., they are intentionally acting against the best interest of their employers).

If you want to engage your employees or your children, you need to shift from tell and reward to inquire.

As soon as you tell me I should or must do something, you trigger a set of neural networks whose purpose is to resist change. I deny, challenge, ignore, argue, or pay lip service to your instructions. I erect a cognitive and emotional wall between us that you can't permeate.

When you offer me rewards or punishments, a similar set of neural circuits begin to fire. Then a slightly different and equally high and strong wall goes up.

With either of these walls, the harder you push against them, the stronger they become.

When you inquire/ask questions, you don't erect the wall. The conversation becomes about them, not about what you want or expect.

Using the four most powerful questions, you can walk me through a process of self-discovery. This process first focuses on what I want—what truly motivates me.

When I ask people that first question—What do you want?—the most common responses are:

- That's a really good question. It's been a long time since I really thought about that.
- You know I want a good _____.

Either response is an admission they no longer know what they want or have a very vague notion lacking a clear definition.

Once they are clear about what they want, they can assess for themselves if what they are doing is working or not. Again, you're not telling them. They are telling themselves.

Finally, they have to grapple with their plan. Often they don't have one or the plan is to work harder doing what isn't really getting them what they want in the first place.

Here's a real-life example. It's performance review time at a major company. The manager is Sheryl, and the person being reviewed is Sawyer. This is the fourth time they have done a performance review. For four years in a row, Sheryl has given Sawyer a 4 out of 5 score. She has also not put Sawyer up for promotion. Let's pick up near the end of the conversation in Sheryl's office.

Sheryl: "Sawyer, please tell me what it is you want?"

Sawyer (barely able to keep from screaming): "You're kidding, right? I want to and deserve to be promoted!"

Sheryl: "You want to be promoted. Ok. Exactly what are you doing to get promoted?"

Sawyer (totally exasperated): "What I have done every year for four years. I do exactly what I am asked to do. I hit every performance objective you set for me."

Sheryl: "To get promoted you do everything asked and hit every target set for you. How is that working?"

Sawyer: "I've done it four years in a row, and you've never agreed to put me up for promotion. So it's not working at all!"

Sheryl: "So what's your plan?"

Sawyer: "For the fifth year in a row, I will do everything asked and hit every target."

Sheryl: "You want to get promoted. You do everything you are asked to, and you hit every objective. This hasn't worked for four years. Your plan is to do exactly the same thing in the coming year. Have I got that right?"

Sawyer: "That doesn't make any sense, does it? I need a new plan."

Sheryl: "Would you like to talk about a new plan that will lead to my putting you up for promotion?"

Sawyer: "Yes, I would."

Sheryl: "You are absolutely right. You have always done everything asked and hit your objectives. You are great at your current job. To get promoted you have to do more than asked and surpass your objectives."

Sheryl had told Sawyer for four years—and many more times than during the annual performance review—that he needed to do more than asked and surpass his objectives to get promoted. She was in "tell" mode, which triggered Sawyer's neural circuits to throw up the walls of resistance. Using the four most powerful questions, Sheryl got Sawyer engaged with himself.

She put him up for promotion halfway through his fifth year. A true story. You can't make this stuff up!

As I write this, the rate of new COVID-19 infections across the United States has hit a new high— 402,270 cases in a single day.. Yet the news and social media are replete with pictures, videos, and reports of people by the thousands not wearing masks, not washing hands, and not maintaining social distancing. Public health authorities and medical providers are beyond frustrated at the inability to get people to follow these few behaviors. If you've ever tried to get someone to wear a mask, you've probably been met with rude gestures or expletives I choose not to write here. What if we tried the four most powerful questions?

Here's a conversation between me and someone—let's call her Joelle—not wearing a mask. I saw her yesterday in the grocery store. She was clearly in the late stages of pregnancy and was neither wearing a mask nor keeping social distancing.

Me: "Hi, how are you doing?"

Joelle: "Uhhh. It's hot and uncomfortable. I can hardly walk and can't wait for my boy to come."

Me: "Congratulations! What do you want for your son and yourself?"

Joelle: "I want things to be back to normal. I want to live our lives without all this worry and inconvenience."

Me: "I understand. So what are you doing to make that happen?"

Joelle: "I've just started to chill. I'm not going to drive myself and my family crazy with all these precautions that don't mean anything. I'm not wearing a mask, and I'm not going to stress about being closer than six feet to another human being."

Me: "How is that working?"

Joelle: "How's it working? Look around at all these people gawking at me, gossiping about the "crazy pregnant lady" and pointing fingers."

Me: "So if I hear you right, instead of feeling better not stressing about masks and stuff, you're actually more upset because of how people are reacting to you?"

Joelle: "You know I was so pissed off at these people I hadn't thought about it that way."

Me: "So what's your plan?"

Joelle: "I don't know. Maybe it's easier just to go along and do what the 'experts' tell us. At least with a mask on I don't get gawked at. And keeping six feet away from these people seems like a good idea for lots of reasons."

A little while later I saw Joelle in the neighborhood pharmacy. She was wearing a mask.

You may be thinking, okay but she's wearing a mask and keeping social distance for the wrong reasons! That may be true but does it matter? As long as people follow the precautions, we're all safer and we'll get through the pandemic faster.

If I had "joined the crowd" giving her a hard time for her behavior, I would have been perceived as a threat and triggered an amygdala hijacking (as we discussed in Chapter 2). She might have gone running from the store in tremendous anger at "those people," more convinced than ever that following the precautions is an unnecessary inconvenience. Remember: When people are stressed, they are more likely to amplify their behavior, not change it. In this case Joelle's anger would have become greater and her resistance to precautions stronger.

Instead, she became compliant—at least for a bit. She also became more open to hearing new information and any new science about the need to follow precautions.

She may also be experiencing a stressful conflict called cognitive dissonance, which was first identified by Leon Festinger[37] in the late 1950s. The basis of the stress is that a person's actions are inconsistent with their beliefs and/or self-image. Here's how it may work with Joelle.

Joelle is now publicly and voluntarily following precautions. She has a positive self-image of herself as someone who is smart, a good parent with good values, and who makes good decisions and has great inner strength. She believes that following the precautions is an unnecessary inconvenience. Voluntarily following the precautions is in conflict with both her self-image and her beliefs. She can't change her behavior because it was public, and she wasn't forced or coerced into following precautions. She doesn't want to change her self-image (i.e., change her image as someone who doesn't make good decisions and doesn't have great inner strength). The only thing she can change is her belief. She'll likely do that because the inconsistency is emotionally stressful.

Once she changes her belief, she will be more likely to stay compliant with the precautions to avoid any future inconsistency between self-image and her beliefs and behaviors.

If she had been coerced into changing her behavior, there would be no conflict. Being forced to do something against your beliefs doesn't create conflict. Therefore, she would be less likely to continue to follow the precautions.

The bottom line: The four most powerful questions may motivate people to change for the long term whereas punishments and penalties will only create change for a short period.

The Four Most Powerful Questions Tool

Trying to survive in the thin air of COVID-19 and amid racial and social injustice and financial needs keeps us focused on surviving rather than thriving. Yet, this is the perfect time for all of us to recreate our set of balanced goals. Everything we were used to—including all the things that have kept us distracted from focusing on what's important—is no longer. It's all been left back in the phase of Endings. We can't go back to or reopen what was because it no longer exists. So while we're in this tremendous uncertainty, it's the perfect time to define how we want to live our lives going forward into New Beginnings.

Even before this time of tremendous uncertainty, most of us didn't find the time to really think through what we want out of life. At best, we ended up with broad generalizations. For instance, "I want to have a life partner and adopt two children" sounds like a fair beginning. What are the characteristics of the life partner you desire? Where will you adopt the children from? Will they be eight or nine years old? Does race or ethnicity matter to you? If you don't find a life partner, do you still want to adopt?

Clarity about what we want is essential in having a balanced life. If we don't know what we want from each life arena, it is very difficult to make tradeoffs, which is one reason many of us become addicted to work and burn out. If we don't know what else we want to pursue—in detail—then it's hard to turn off work for a while and pursue what we want outside of work.

If you have a partner and/or child, completing this separately and then sharing your answers can be a very worthwhile exercise.

The tool walks you through a process of asking the four most powerful questions in terms of what you want and are doing with regard to family, health, spirituality, community, and profession.

The process works for the same reasons as using the four most powerful questions approach because it generates an internal conversation rather than resistance.

The difference is the tool applies the four most powerful questions across the five life arenas. It fosters a balanced life because it takes you beyond the world of work. You end up with a more broad and complete view of what you want from all aspects of your life.

It is important to realize what the tool doesn't do. It doesn't lead you to spending equal amounts of time in each life arena. If you work, that will probably be the area in which you spend most of your time and energy. If you are a single parent, your family may be the area in which you spend most of your time.

What the tool does do is clarify what you want in each arena and a reasonable plan for moving in that direction. The answer to "what's your plan?" should be fairly simple in the majority of life arenas. I eat my own cooking so let me share my objectives and plans created by using these tools over the years.

Spirituality

What do I want? A deeper understanding of some of the world's religions.

What am I doing? I occasionally watch a TED Talk or read something.

How is that working? It's not.

What's your plan? For one year I decided I would learn something new about Buddhism each week. Sunday morning is when I reviewed my progress against my goals. If during the week I hadn't learned something new about Buddhism, I simply did a Google search on Buddhism and watched a TED Talk or read a book chapter or article. It took anywhere from 15 minutes to an hour. By the end of the year I had a deeper understanding of Buddhism.

The following three years I focused on Hinduism, Islam, and Judaism.

Health

What do I want? To be in better shape.

What am I doing? I exercise sporadically and do some yoga.

How is that working? I'm still overweight.

What's your plan? Find a new diet.

This didn't work. I mean for years it didn't work. Remember: The four most powerful questions and the four most powerful questions tool create the greatest chance that someone will become motivated to change. It is not a guarantee. The truth is I didn't really care enough.

As with all resilience behaviors, the key is to practice them consistently so they become your automatic response in relevant situations.

My wife and I were sitting in the audience as our granddaughter, Mackenzie, was graduating from eighth grade and moving into her first year of high school. At the end of the ceremony, the high school principal came on stage and inducted the Class of 2021 into the high school. My mind immediately went to "Mackenzie is going to be in the Class of 2025 in college. She'll just be beginning her adult life. I'll be 69."

What do I want? I want to be part of her life well beyond college graduation. I want to be active and doing things with her.

What am I doing? Nothing that will make sure I'm healthy into my 80s and hopefully 90s.

How's that working? Oh crap.

What's my plan? I'm going to lose weight and get my blood pressure, cholesterol, and uric acid (high uric acid causes gout) down. I'm going to lose weight by changing the way I eat, not dieting.

A year later I had lost 26 pounds. My blood pressure and cholesterol were normal. I was taken off the statins for cholesterol, and my blood pressure meds were reduced. My uric acid levels were below normal—a very good thing for someone with a history of gout. I had the best physical exam results since college.

What happened was watching Mackenzie on stage triggered the four most powerful questions in the family arena. Family is something I care deeply about. The questioning process motivated me to lose weight and improve my health because that is the only way to get what I want in the family arena.

Family

What do I want? I want to become even closer to my wife and daughters, sons-in-law, and grandkids. Closer means having more conversations and sharing things.

What am I doing? Even though I make my living teaching, coaching, and working intensely with people, I'm a really strong introvert. I like to be alone, which directly conflicts with my desire to become closer to my family.

How's that working? It's not.

What's my plan? I'm going to specifically work on spending more time with my family members. With my wife I'm going to have coffee with her every morning when she first wakes up. As I write, I think I'm building a pretty good track record at this. With the rest of my family, I'm going to accept their help in the kitchen. I do most of the cooking—I enjoy it, and it gives me alone time. My kids and grandkids are always asking: "Need any help, Dad?" and "Anything I can do Dad?" My answer has traditionally been: "No, I got it." Going forward it's going to be: "Yeah, could you...?" so we'll spend time cooking together.

Community

What do I want? I want to make a difference to causes I care about. I don't want to do that by responding to disasters anymore.

What am I doing? I'm volunteering with our church's Homeless Ministry. I run the annual distribution of warm hats, gloves, and socks. I support the Children's Learning Centers of Fairfield County with pro bono coaching and training. I serve on the Board of Tuesday's Children. I work to help Levo International expand their efforts in using hydroponic farming to create food and economic security for the world's poorest.

How's that working? I think it's working really well.

What's my plan? Keep doing what I'm doing and be careful not to take on too much more.

Profession

What do I want? Quite frankly, I'm torn between taking a senior corporate job I'm being offered and continuing to devote myself to the building of resilience among people, organizations, and communities.

What am I doing? Right now in the midst of Uncertainty I'm very focused on my resilience work. At the same time I took on a consulting assignment with my potential employer.

How's it working? It's working well. I'm rewarded by both, and I'm not pushing a decision until I'm sure where I want to be in New Beginnings.

What's my plan? Keep working on both until I'm clear about what I really want.

CHAPTER 10

ENGAGING IN A HIGHER PURPOSE

E ngaging in a higher purpose means connecting to the greater good you serve and sharing that connection with others. It is using your strengths, talents, resources, and energy to contribute to something greater than yourself.

First, we will discuss how to build this factor and then discuss why and how it works.

The Routine

There are six behaviors to practice that strengthen engaging in a higher purpose:

1. Find your higher purpose.
2. Use the four most powerful questions tool.
3. Engage in your higher purpose.
4. Engage in storytelling.
5. Do some visioning.
6. Engage yourself.

Find Your Higher Purpose

Even if you already know what your higher purpose is, completing this process can be very helpful in engaging with it.

Identifying Your Signature Strengths

- Researchers at the University of Pennsylvania's Positive Psychology Center have identified 24 universal strengths. For each of us, our five strongest are our signature strengths.
- To identify your signature strengths, take the free Brief Strengths Test by going to this website: https://www.authentichappiness. sas.upenn.edu/questionnaires/ brief-strengths-test.
- After you take the survey, you will receive a list of the 24 universal strengths in rank order. The first five are your signature strengths.

Identifying Possible Higher Purposes to Engage In

Now you have two options:

1. Go back to Chapter 9: Balanced Goal-Setting and review the objectives (the answer to the first of the four most powerful questions) you set for each of your life arenas (i.e., family, community, health, spirituality, and profession/career).
   - Does your objective in any life arena involve serving a higher purpose?
   - If so, how can you improve your plan to achieve this objective by leveraging or making greater use of your signature strengths?
   - Imagine yourself actually using your signature strengths to achieve your higher purpose.
   - How do you feel?
     - o If you feel strong positive emotions (e.g., fulfillment, energy, excitement, peace, joy,

accomplishment), then activate your plan for 90 days.

- o After 90 days review how well you followed your plan and the emotions you've experienced, which will tell you whether to continue engaging in this higher purpose or to start the process over to try engaging in a different higher purpose.

2. Consider your signature strengths and what higher purposes you could use them to engage in.

- Start by just listing as many ideas as you can.
- If you find that difficult, go back to Chapter 8: Agility and use:
  - o Framing/reframing
  - o Modified triggered brain walking
- Write your five signature strengths on five sheets of paper.
- Use each strength as a trigger for ideas about possible higher purposes to engage with.
  - o The modification to the technique is you are doing this by yourself, not in a group.
- If you come up with a list of signature strengths and are having difficulty selecting one, use the aligning options technique

Trying Out Your Higher Purpose

Once you've selected a higher purpose in which to engage, give yourself 90 days to try it out. If after 90 days you find yourself feeling positive emotions as you engage in your higher purpose, then stick with it. If after 90 days you feel neutral or negative emotions as you engage in your higher purpose, it is probably best to take another one from your list of possibilities and read the Engage Yourself section in this chapter.

Use the Four Most Powerful Questions Tool

This tool is a key component of building balanced goal-setting. If you have already completed it, that's great! Review it every week or so. If you haven't completed it, go to page 114 and do so.

Engage in Your Higher Purpose

Find ways to use your five signature strengths to engage with your higher purpose. You can find ways to do this in any arena of your life: career, family, community, spirituality, or health.

For example, you work for a major medical center, which is linked to your higher purpose in contributing to people's health and recovery from illness. Suppose your strongest signature strength is creativity. The core of this strength is thinking of new ways to do things. New isn't enough. To leverage your creativity strength, the new ideas must be of practical value or use—new ideas that make a positive contribution to yourself and others.

Also suppose you are an accountant working in the audit department. You have a highly routinized job. Your day-to-day work may not allow for creativity—possibly even forbidding it.

To engage in your higher purpose by using your creativity, you could look for opportunities to participate on task forces or teams looking to improve the patient experience within the medical center or to improve some important internal processes. You could seek training in Six Sigma to ensure you are sought after for such assignments.

Perhaps your department is severely understaffed. As a practical matter, you don't have the time to take on additional assignments. In this situation the key is to find opportunities to use your creativity in another part of your life.

For example, you could volunteer with a food pantry or meals on wheels program, seeking to improve the nutrition of those in need. The key is not to volunteer to help with the organization's accounting needs because that will not give you an opportunity to use your creativity. You could volunteer to find new ways to attract more volunteers, additional restaurants that can contribute leftovers, or a new way to raise funds. The key is to make sure your volunteer role allows you to be creative.

Engage in Storytelling

Storytelling is just that. Tell stories about how you engage in your higher purpose. Stories bring things to life for the listener and the teller.

1. Begin by keeping a story journal, which is a notebook you keep handy to jot down stories.
   - Write down stories that are told to you—particularly when you are first exploring your higher purpose.
   - Most important are the stories that you experience in serving your higher purpose.
2. On a regular basis sit down with your story journal and review the stories you have jotted down.
   - Select a story to craft.
   - Decide who you want to tell the story to. For example,
     o Friends who might want to join the organization or activity you are involved in to serve your higher purpose
     o People who might benefit from the services provided by your organization
     o Someone who might publicize your organization's good works
   - In one statement write the core message you are trying to convey.
   - Identify the conflict or challenge that is central to the story.
     o Write the narrative of the story.
   - Keep it concise.
   - Start with a sentence that grabs the attention of your audience.
   - Use simple and straightforward language.
   - Don't make it all about you.

3. Practice your stories.
   - Rehearse in private until the story just flows from you.
   - Practice in front of friends and relatives to get their feedback. Learn from each practice how to improve your story.

For more information on how to tell stories, I strongly recommend reading *What's Your Story?* by my old friend and colleague Craig Wortmann.[38] He's a true master storyteller!

Do Some Visioning

Visualize engaging in your higher purpose by following these steps:

1. Sit quietly.
2. Take a few deep belly breaths (see Chapter 5: Focus).
3. Call to mind the definition of your higher purpose (e.g., I want to make a difference in the lives of the homeless).
4. Visualize/imagine what it will look like when you are engaged in your higher purpose.
   - Imagine the setting.
   - Imagine the people who will be with you.
   - Imagine what you will be doing and what others will be doing.
   - Imagine the difference you will be making.
   - Imagine how it will feel.
5. Practice this once or twice a week.

Engage Yourself

Engaging in a higher purpose is all about two things: getting involved and setting realistic expectations.

- Be realistic about how much time, energy, and resources you can devote to being engaged with your higher purpose.

- o If engaging in your higher purpose is part of your work or family, then the amount of time you can be engaged with your higher purpose may be very substantial.
- o If engaging in your higher purpose demands being more involved with your community or spiritual life, be careful not to overcommit.
- o For instance, if you work full time and are a single parent, realistically, you may only have two or three hours each month to devote to engaging in your higher purpose.
- Get involved with the parts of serving your higher purpose that mean the most to you.
  - o Often that means the parts that allow you to use your signature strengths.

Why and How It Works![39]

Research has proven that there are significant differences between being happy and fulfilled. Happiness comes from experiencing and receiving things that are pleasurable. Fulfillment comes from being engaged with your higher purpose.

According to Martin Seligman, there are actually three types of lives[40]:

- The Pleasant Life: In this life, or perhaps part of your life, happiness is experienced when we enjoy things and experiences. A good dinner, a great movie, or a relaxing day at the beach are all examples of the sources of happiness from The Pleasant Life. The problem with The Pleasant Life is that happiness is not enduring. To stay happy, we need to keep experiencing or receiving more and more things. There is ample evidence that we not only need to keep a steady flow; it has to be of increasingly greater things and experiences to maintain our happiness. The Pleasant Life produces unhappiness when the need for greater and greater pleasures grows. The need for greater and greater pleasures is especially likely to grow when we are under stress.

Certainly, this period of uncertainty is such a circumstance. As we've said earlier, when we are under stress, we tend to amplify existing behaviors. If prior to the current period of uncertainty we sought pleasure in enjoying a glass of wine, eating a fine meal, or playing cards, these behaviors are likely to amplify or increase, possibly leading to a drinking problem, obesity, or a gambling addiction.

- The Good Life: Life fulfillment comes from using your signature strengths to develop mastery in one or more areas. When you are using your signature strengths, you are much more likely to enter a state of flow. Flow was first defined and studied by Mihaly Csikszentmihalyi.[41] During flow, time passes without notice. Your focus is completely on what you are doing. Distractions are shut out. You are highly productive, immersed in your task, and feel like you are expending no effort. You feel fully alive, free from worry, and your concentration is at its peak.

  Athletes call this being in the "zone." Flow is most often achieved when your motivation for being immersed in an activity is for intrinsic gratification. That activity itself is rewarding. That doesn't mean it can't be something for which you get paid. It simply means that your initial attraction was for the intrinsic rewards. Many world-renowned artists, singers, musicians, and athletes first became attracted to their profession because of how it intrinsically made them feel. Making a living by carrying out an activity in which you frequently enter a state of flow is the notion behind sayings such as "If you do what you love, you will never work a day in your life." The Good Life provides a sense of satisfaction that is greater and more enduring than the happiness experienced in The Pleasant Life.

- The Meaningful Life: In this life you use your signature skills specifically to serve a higher purpose, which benefits others. It is similar to The Good Life in that you use and strengthen your signature strengths and are more likely to entire a state of flow. It is a better life because the sense of fulfillment is the greatest and longest lasting.

The degree to which you engage in each type of life has a significant impact on your health. The Pleasant Life is one filled with sources of enjoyment. Research has shown that people who experience a high level of The Pleasant Life have a greater level of physiological stress-related responses.[42] Specifically, these individuals have an increased number of genes that increase the likelihood of inflammation and a decrease in the number of genes that promote the creation of antibodies to fight off infection.

The same research found that high levels of experiencing The Meaningful Life had the opposite effect. Those with high levels of The Meaningful Life also had a lower incidence of symptoms of depression.

In sum, while there is nothing wrong with experiencing pleasurable things, overdoing it poses both physical and emotional health risks. Experiencing The Meaningful Life improves and protects both physical and emotional health.

Engaging in a Higher Purpose Amid Uncertainty

As we discussed in Chapter 1, we are not in the midst of one or two crises. We are in the midst of a growing number of simultaneous crises (see Figure 33).

Figure 33: Systemic Problems in Focus

And, unbelievably, the list seems to be growing. According to *The Wall Street Journal*,[43] there was a sharp rise in shootings and killings over the July 4th holiday weekend in 2020. The New York City Police Department reported 44 shootings with 11 people killed. The City of Chicago had 47 shootings with 87 people injured and 17 fatalities. The City of Atlanta has reported 75+ shootings during this time. Reignited, epidemic gun violence is now added to the mix of crises with which we must deal.

The science is very clear: Engaging in a higher purpose increases your emotional and physical wellness. Added to this, from a social perspective, if we are to move forward together to the phase of New Beginnings, we are each called upon to serve the higher purpose of engaging in solving one of these many crises.

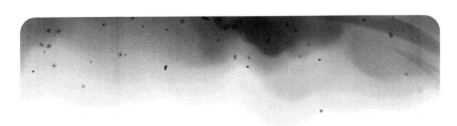

CHAPTER 11

GRIT

G rit is perseverance and passion for long-term goals related to one's passion. It's also courage in managing fear of failure to continue achieving goals related to your passion. It means working tirelessly and driving through inevitable setbacks in pursuing a challenging goal.

The Routine

There are six behaviors to practice in strengthening grit:

1. Find and pursue what interests you.
2. Practice to master what interests you.
3. Envision success.
4. Use positive self-talk.
5. Be optimistic that you will succeed.
6. Surround yourself with gritty people.

Five out of six of these behaviors are contained in other resilience factors! As with all our chapters, I'll begin with how to build the factor and then say more about why and how it works. That way you can get started building your resilience right away.

Find and Pursue What Interests You

Try and experience new things until you begin to feel passionate about achieving or mastering something. You can use the four most powerful questions tool—the discovery version. In this version the four most powerful questions are modified to encourage you to find and explore interests:

1. What am I interested in now?

    If your answer to this first question is "nothing," then develop a plan to learn about and experience new things.

    If you are interested in something now, then continue on to answer the second and third questions.
2. What am I doing to experience more of this or learn more about it?
3. How is that working?
4. What is my plan to experience more of this interest and see if I want to pursue it?

If your answer to the third question is something like "the more I learn, the less I am interested," then your plan—the answer to this fourth question—should be to explore other possible interests.

If your answer to the third question is something like "the more I learn, the more excited I become," then your answer to question four should be to find even more ways of learning about and experiencing it.

Once you find something you have learned and experienced in-depth and find yourself really passionate about achieving or mastering something in that area, move on to the rest of the behaviors.

Remember: The four most powerful questions are part of the balanced goal-setting factor. It helps you identify what you want across various life arenas: career, family, community, health, and spirituality. It's worth looking back at your answers to the four most powerful questions tool in Chapter 9: Balanced Goal-Setting. You can develop grit in any of the life arenas.

Practice to Master What Interests You

- Find as many ways as possible to apply the knowledge and practice the skills related to your passion.
    - o Find ways to do this every day. If your current job or studies don't permit it, then find other outlets to do so. Maybe you can volunteer or get an unpaid internship or take increasingly challenging courses.
- As you practice to master your passion, keep increasing the difficulty of your practice sessions.
    - o If you're mastering a field of mathematics, increase the difficulty of the problems you must solve.
    - o If you're mastering an instrument, then increase the difficulty and complexity of the music you practice.
- As you practice make sure you are getting feedback on how you're doing from tests, colleagues, teachers, and customers or other end users. Most importantly, get feedback from yourself. To do this, practice the resilience factor of self-reflection every day (see Chapter 13).

Envision Success

Visualize achieving mastery of your passion by following these steps:

1. Sit quietly.
2. Take a few deep belly breaths (see Chapter 5: Focus).
3. Call to mind the definition of your passion (e.g., I want to be a master baker).
4. Visualize/imagine what it will look like when you are practicing mastering your passion.
    - Imagine the setting.
    - Imagine the people who will be with you.
    - Imagine what you will be doing and what others will be doing.
    - Imagine the challenges that will be hard to overcome.

- Imagine the failures and disappointments you will face along the way.
- See yourself overcoming difficult challenges, failures, and disappointments.
- Imagine how you will feel during each part of your vision of achieving mastery.

5. Practice this every day before you begin practicing.

Use Positive Self-Talk

- Create a list of positive affirmations, such as these examples:
  - o I will succeed.
  - o I will push through my frustration.
  - o I have the talent and skill to succeed.
  - o I am going to put in the effort to master this.
  - o I will overcome setbacks and disappointments.
- Pay attention to the "chatter" and negative "self-talk" in your head.
- When you notice you are thinking negatively, quickly repeat one of your affirmations three times.
- Do this every time your mind starts to focus on negative self-talk.

Be Optimistic That You Will Succeed

Using our framework, build your Pragmatic Optimism—the belief that the future will be better in part because of what you do. Use the Pragmatic Optimism routine daily.

Whenever you face a setback in mastering your passion (and we all do), make sure to answer a modified version of the three Pragmatic Optimism questions:

1. Will I ever be able to master (my passion)?
   - Yes, with enough practice I will master (my passion).

2. Does it affect everything that is important to me in my life?
   - No.
3. How can I use my skills, knowledge, and experiences to find a way forward?
   - Applying my talent with great effort will create skills (i.e., Talent X Effort = Skill).
   - Applying my skill with great effort will lead to achievement (i.e., Skill X Effort = Achievement).[44]

Join A Gritty Group

Build a support network of people who are pursuing their passion. Surround yourself with people who master something truly important to them. They don't have to be passionate about the same thing you are; you just need people who are committed to being gritty in pursuit of something meaningful.

Again, you can build your grit by practicing the behaviors that develop another resilience factor—in this case that factor is empathy. In particular, you can find people who are passionate and gritty by having empathic conversations with people.

The empathic conversation has the following five behaviors:

1. Be curious: Ask questions.
2. Listen intently to words, tone, and body language.
3. Acknowledge what you hear. Let people know what they said means to you.
4. Stay open: Don't interrupt or shut down when you hear things you don't agree with.
5. Be yourself: Be comfortable talking about you.

Why and How It Works!

Angela Duckworth[45] and her colleagues have proven that those with higher levels of grit achieve more than those of similar talent who are lower on grit. In other words, high achievement is the result of both talent and intense, focused, long-term effort to achieve a goal. Duckworth and colleagues point out that hard work and talent are widely understood as contributing to success. Grit sheds light on the fact that long-term pursuit of the same goals and objectives is really what distinguishes those high on grit and their high levels of achievement.

The research also found that grit increases with age, which supports the idea that you can intentionally increase your level of grit by following the routine described above.

So why is the length of time you pursue your passion so important? Simply put, success takes time.

Here are some examples.

Recently I was a guest lecturer at CalTech. I had the opporunity to listen to, speak with, and enjoy a tour of CalTech's Humanoid Robotics Lab given by Professor Aaron Ames. Professor Ames and his team of graduate students design, build, and test robots and prostheses. What became clear during this experience was the painstaking nature of developing even the most routine of human movements in a working robot. The number and length of mathematical calculations are stunning. It also became clear that he and his team will be able to fulfill their passion for many, many years to come.

Figure 34: Photo by Bryan Mattimore, Chief Idea Guy @ The Growth Engine

Figure 34 is a photo of a member of Aaron's team demonstrating an exoskeleton that one day will enable people who have lost the ability to walk to do so.

What happens when—through our grit—we eventually achieve the goals we have been so passionate about? It's likely that you can find one or more new passions and goals to pursue by tapping into your grit. In fact, finding a new passion and focus for your grit may be an essential ingredient to continued happiness and fulfillment.

I have the privilege of being an executive coach to a number of highly successful leaders of corporations, medical centers, and nonprofit organizations. Often I am working with them as they are nearing the end of their first career. These are people with huge passions and very high grit. Most often they have focused on rising to the top of their profession or major organization since adolescence. They have achieved what they set out to—and many times more.

The question now becomes what next?, which really means what can I be passionate about? Where can I put my grit to good use? How can I stay relevant?

Those who focus on engaging in a (new) higher purpose as the basis for refocusing their grit live highly productive lives for decades—decades when they often have a tremendous impact on the lives of others.

Those who don't fully engage in a process we might call "passion and grit redirection" run a high risk of sadness, unfulfillment, and even depression. They enter retirement (better viewed as "The Next Chapter") with vague ideas such as "I'll sit on a few boards" or "I'd like to teach" or "I think I'll consult" or "we'll travel" and finally "we'll spend time with the kids and grandkids." These sound like bromides from the 1960s television show *The Adventures of Ozzie and Harriet*. To be fair, in the early 1960s vague plans of what to do in retirement might not have been so bad. After all, the average male retired at 65 years old and lived to the age of 66.6 years.

That's a far cry from today when the life expectancy is, on average, 80 years of age. Retirement can easily now be as much as or more than 25 percent of your life. In this era happiness and health require "passion and grit redirection."

Bill and Melinda Gates provide another amazing example of the power of "passion and grit redirection." In 2011 Bill read a rarely read report from the World Health Organization that documented the fact that fully 40 percent of the world's population has no access to sanitary systems, meaning they defecate in holes in the ground, trenches that lead to fresh water sources, or out in the open. This horrific situation ignited the passion of both Bill and Melinda so they directed their grit to solve the problem. At the end of 2018, The Bill and Melinda Gates Foundation had donated over $200 million; Bill and Melinda have been creating awareness and driving innovation for seven years. As I write this, innovations are improving sanitation around the world while producing energy and clean water. There is still a long way to go. It seems the Gates have the grit to see it through.

If you're interested in "passion and grit redirection," take a lesson from Bill Gates. He reads broadly, deeply, and incessantly. That's one way you uncover new passions and give yourself the opportunity to engage in a higher purpose and put your grit to great use.

In this environment with its growing number of simultaneous crises that have caused us to abandon much of what we knew as "living normally," there are a number of bright spots. All the challenges we face in this period of unimaginable uncertainty create new opportunities to explore and find new passions—passions that never existed before that will be critical for us to move forward into the phase of New Beginnings. For example, I was talking to an old friend a few days ago. His son is 33 years old and had a good job with an insurance company. Good salary, good future, and nothing but boredom on the horizon! Seeing all the uncertainty around us, he began to become passionate about software and applications development. He sees them as essential in navigating out of uncertainty and creating New Beginnings. So he quit his full-time job (yes, amid massive unemployment) and enrolled in a software development program. He will take classes and complete challenging assignments from 9 a.m. to 7 p.m., six days a week for 16 weeks. He'll be expected to do homework most of each Sunday. He will get enough practice, amid a group of gritty individuals, to master programming and move forward with his passion.

A woman I know just had her first child. She and her husband have both been off for three months on childcare leave. In a month she had planned to return to a well-paying job in doing important work with a clear career path. She's not going back. She's decided being on-call 24/7 isn't worth the cost. Her new passion is being a parent. She's exploring other careers that allow her to master that.

Now let's examine why each of the behaviors in the routine works to develop grit.

Find and Pursue What Interests You

Duckworth talks about how powerful influencers, such as our parents, can direct us toward practical goals—especially when it comes to professions. In fact, she shares her father's experience as a boy in China.[46] Her grandparents owned a textile plant. Therefore, they directed each of their sons to master part of the textile manufacturing process. Her father's passion was history, which he had to abandon in favor of a degree in chemistry.

My own father wanted me to become an attorney—a goal I pursued until I was accepted at Fordham Law School with a partial scholarship. From my junior year in high school I had been volunteering with a crisis line and working in various kinds of programs to improve the emotional health of children and adolescents. Through those experiences I found my passions, which won out when I elected to pursue my PhD rather than my JD.

Trying new experiences is simply the best way of identifying what you are passionate about.

Practice to Master What Interests You

Developing resilience is based upon the scientific knowledge of brain plasticity and the ability to rewire the brain to do things—whether they are cognitive or physical. As you practice and consistently increase the challenge level of your sessions, you will continually increase the complexity and durability of neural networks that enable mastery.

Envision Success

By visioning your journey to mastery, you rewire the brain. Specifically, you rewire the brain to expect challenges, failures, and disappointments as signals of progress. You also wire in practical responses to overcome them. Visioning creates neural learning that enables you to persevere until success.

Use Positive Self-Talk

This is similar to how the gratitude exercise (see Chapter 4: Pragmatic Optimism) counters the amygdala's efforts to keep us in fight-or-flight mode when any stress is perceived. A lot of us have consistently received messages during our lives that we:

- Aren't good enough
- Haven't "got what it takes"
- Won't amount to anything
- Never do anything right

Long after the people who said these words to us are no longer around, we "hear" them in our mind as they have been hard-wired into our brains. Positive self-talk counters these messages. Over time the positive self-talk neural networks you build will be stronger than the negative ones. At that point your brain will pare down or delete the negative self-talk networks.

Be Optimistic That You Will Succeed

As we discussed in Chapter 4: Pragmatic Optimism – The First Factor To Concentrate On, when something bad happens many people experience three emotional reactions. These reactions happen quickly, often simultaneously, and can quickly overwhelm us. They can feel like tremendous waves hitting you all at once, interfering with your ability to breathe, take in information, or see a way forward. When you practice mastering your passion and developing your grit, bad things are bound to happen along the way. You will have practice sessions that feel disastrous. You will receive feedback from others that your mastery is not moving forward smoothly.

So it's critical that you answer this modified version of the three Pragmatic Optimism questions. You want to wire your brain to respond to setbacks and disappointments with automatic thoughts:

- This will not last forever; I will master my passion.
- It doesn't impact everything in my life; all is not at risk.
- I will apply two formulas to achieve mastery
  - o Talent X Effort = Skill
  - o Skill X Effort = Achievement[47]

Surrounding Yourself With Gritty People

This triggers your competitive neural networks to motivate you to move forward. It also provides empathetic social support (i.e., people who really get you). Finally, it also wires your brain to see the experience of mastery as normal, not extraordinary. All the signals you receive from other gritty folks make you feel encouraging emotions such as fulfillment and joy, not discouraging emotions such as failure, sadness, and loneliness.

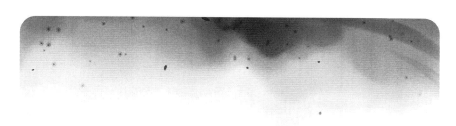

CHAPTER 12

SELF-CONTROL

S elf-control limits distractions, avoids multitasking, and makes conscious choices under pressure possible. It also helps control expression of emotions to maintain relationships and personal performance.

The Routine

There are five behaviors to practice in strengthening self-control:

1. Set the stage.
2. Take away or block temptations.
3. Surf the urge.
4. S.T.O.P.
5. Building new habits.

Set the Stage

This behavior is simply explicitly stating for yourself what you want to accomplish by building your self-control. Just write down your objective. Some examples:

- Have 30 minutes a day to think about long-term challenges.
- Lose 10 pounds.

- Exercise for 20 minutes each day.
- Spend an hour with my children before bedtime.

For me, my goal in improving my self-control was to complete this book!

Take Away or Block Temptations

This behavior is to remove short-term distractions/temptations in advance and to make working toward long-term objectives easier.

Here are some examples:

You know that checking your emails and texts before getting out of bed can reduce your productivity for the day (see Chapter 4: Focus). If you keep your smartphone at your bedside, when you wake up you will have to fight the urge to pick it up and start multitasking. If you keep your smartphone in a drawer by the front door, you remove the temptation (at least from the bedroom).

Suppose you are on a diet and want to limit carbohydrates and increase fruits. When shopping you don't buy bread, potatoes, and other high-carb foods. You do buy plenty of fresh fruit. At home you put the fruit out in bowls in several rooms such as your home office, family room, and kitchen.

If you want to practice the keyboard and not binge watch shows, put the keyboard in the center of the family room and put the remote in a drawer in the kitchen.

Manipulating our surroundings to advantage is, in fact, a highly effective form of self-control.

Surf the Urge

Whenever you are faced with the temptation to be distracted from your longer-term goal (e.g., answer emails in the middle of drafting a report; eat cookies late at night; smoke a cigarette), simply do the following:

1. Notice the temptation and accept that you are craving it.

2. Take one mindful (deep, slow) breath.
3. Focus on one thing you can do to keep moving toward your longer-term goal.
   - Examples: Look up some information for the report you are writing instead of checking email. Take a five-minute walk instead of going to the kitchen where the cookies are.
4. Take the action to move toward your longer-term goal.
5. Notice how as you move toward your longer-term goal or simply distract yourself from the temptation, your craving subsides.

S.T.O.P.

Whenever you are tempted to give into a craving, do the following:

1. Stop what you are doing
2. Take a mindful breath (focus your attention on taking a slow, deep breath).
3. Observe what you are doing and what you are thinking.
4. Proceed to keep doing what you are doing or give in to the craving.

Building New Habits

Complete the Power of Habit worksheet (see Figure 35).

- Identify an existing habit that creates stress, lowers productivity, or reduces the fulfillment you get from your work.
- In detail, describe the cue, routine, and reward. Take your time to really understand each of these.
- Next, identify a new routine (e.g., a resilience behavior) to replace the routine in the existing habit.
- Complete this process for three or four existing habits.
- Select one new habit to build.

- Transfer your new habit to the power of habit card.
  - o   Post it in a highly visible place.
- Focus only on this habit until it becomes automatic.
- Then select your next new habit to develop.

The Power Of Habit Worksheet (EXAMPLES)		
Cue	Routine	Reward
Existing Habit: Email pops up.	Check emails. Read. Don't respond.	• Reduction in pressure of working on multiple assignments. • False sense of being in control.
New Habit: Email pops up.	Use STOP technique	• Real sense of control. • Improved focus relieves pressure of multiple assignments
Existing Habit: New assignment received	Begin working on solution without clear criteria	Feeling of movement forward
New Habit: New assignment received	Use Aligning Options Tool	Movement forward
Existing Habit: Boss provides criticism of recent deliverable	Vent with colleagues, friends. Sharing fear of damage to career	Social support and sympathy
New Habit: Boss provides criticism of recent deliverable	Use The Practicing Optimism Tool.	Social support, guidance, collaboration, confidence

THRIVING IN THIN AIR

Existing Habit: Colleagues grumbling about company and workload	Join in	Feelings of validation and belonging.
New Habit: Colleagues grumbling about company and workload	Intentionally spend time with optimistic colleagues	Feelings of validation and belonging and motivation to move forward
Existing Habit: Feeling unfulfilled by work	Focus on pleasant activities	Temporary feelings of relief when engaged in pleasant activities
New Habit: Feeling unfulfilled by work	Complete or review completed The Four Most Powerful Questions Tool	Feelings of accomplishment and meaning from multiple areas of life

The Power Of Habit Worksheet		
Cue	Routine	Reward
Existing Habit:		
New Habit:		
Existing Habit:		

New Habit:		
Existing Habit:		
New Habit:		
Existing Habit:		

Figure 35: The Power of Habit Worksheet

Why and How It Works!

Around the globe people rate themselves lower on self-control than most other aspects of character such as kindness, commitment, and curiosity.[50] Self-control is choosing between two conflicting choices. Many labels have been used over the years to identify these two choices. We will use immediate vs. long-term. The immediate choice gives us instant satisfaction or gratification. The long-term choice will require more time and perhaps work to gain satisfaction. The pull or tension to take the immediate choice is often stronger—at least in the moment—than the long-term choice. For example, our desire to eat or drink sweet things is hard-wired in our brains. When searching for edible foods in nature, people needed a rapid way to identify food worth eating and safe to eat. Things that taste sweet are often high in calories and a source of quick energy. They also are generally not poisonous.

When we eat something sweet that is high in sugar, the brain produces large amounts of dopamine. Dopamine creates similar sensations to opiates. We often call this a "sugar rush." That's a powerful and immediate reward for falling off our diet! Over time eating and drinking sugar actually becomes addictive. The immediate surge of dopamine is much more rewarding than being able to tell ourselves we did well by avoiding temptation—at least in the moment.

While Plato didn't know the neurologic and physiologic reasons why we give in to immediate temptations, he did understand the tremendous difficulty in resisting them. He conceived of people as being in a chariot being pulled by two horses. The first was the noble, white horse—the horse that was consistently pulling us toward our long-term objectives. The black horse was wild and unpredictable. When the black horse saw something it craved, it could muster enough energy to pull the white horse off course in pursuit of its craving. Our challenge was to pull hard on the reins to keep the white horse on track and pull the black horse back on course. Plato's analogy paints a really clear picture of the energy needed to resist temptations and craving.

Set the stage behaviors help us resist cravings by making sure that we and our white horse are clear on the long-term path we want to take and what we want to achieve. Without this our focus and the white horses won't be on the right spot on the horizon.

Take away or block temptation behaviors work because they are like putting blinders on our black horse. When the black horse literally can't see a temptation or the way to get to it, it stays—relatively—calm and on track. Another way to understand this is that when we don't perceive a temptation or see it as difficult to attain, the hard wiring in our brain that craves it is less likely to be triggered.

Surf the urge behaviors work because they help push your black horse past the point where it can seize the temptation. Essentially, the black horse runs out of energy as you and the white horse are aligned in resisting the black horse's efforts. Neurologically, the neural circuits that create and maintain the craving will eventually stop firing if you can resist the temptation by distracting yourself or avoiding the temptation for just a few minutes.

S.T.O.P. behaviors work because they are like pulling hard on the reins and yelling "Whoa!"—bringing you and your horses to a halt. They allow you to fully assess the situation and the choices you face.

Neurologically, you are calming down the circuits that fire to create the craving and activating the circuits in your frontal lobe that carry out critical thinking and decision-making.

Building New Habits

On average, 40 percent of what you do every day is a result of established "hard-wired" habits. They are hard-wired because they are enabled by neural networks within your brain. These networks cause you to begin a set of behaviors as soon as a related cue is perceived. You carry out the behaviors without thinking or making a decision. By executing the set of behaviors you reward yourself in any number of ways. Figure 34 illustrates the pattern of a habit.

Figure 36: Habit Building Pattern

The only way to replace an existing habit is to create one that is stronger. A new habit becomes stronger than an existing habit through repetition. Repetition builds a new neural network that fires in response to the cue before the old/existing habit network. The new habit must be triggered by the old cue and provide the same reward(s).[51]

In summary, the key to establishing a new habit is to keep the same cue and reward as the old habit and replace the routine.

As you can see, avoiding and resisting distractions and temptations requires a lot of emotional and cognitive control. That control expends energy. That's why it's easier to resist temptation when you are fully rested than when you are tired. The key to self-control is getting adequate sleep on a regular basis. One easy way to know if you are getting enough sleep is if you find yourself waking up before the alarm goes off—feeling refreshed and ready to go.

Ideally, you want to structure your day so that when you are most likely to be tired you are in situations where you are less tempted to give in to cravings. For example, the later I am awake, the more I crave unhealthy snacks. Going up to bed to read takes me physically away from the snacks and distracts me from the craving.

At this point the pandemic has been in the United States for over a year. From a resilience point of view, that's more than the 60 to 70 days it takes for any consistent behavior to rewire our brains. Under stress, many limitations and a complete disruption to our normal schedules allows new, unhealthy habits to easily take hold. For example, a few weeks ago I had an appointment with my internist. While the nurse was taking my blood pressure, temperature, and weight, she commented: "You're doing well. The average person we see has gained 10 pounds since the pandemic."

It's a good time to create a list of new habits. Are you eating differently? Are you watching more "news" and finding yourself anxious? Are you getting less exercise? Once you have created this list, you may want to identify several new habits that you want to rewire.

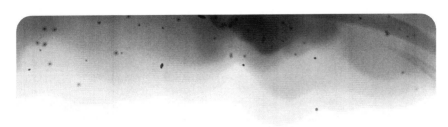

CHAPTER 13

SELF-REFLECTION

Self-reflection is the ability to objectively review past behaviors, attitudes, perspectives, and results and then to learn from this review. It results in personal growth and changes in behavior.

The Routine

Self-reflection has the simplest routine of any of the 10 resilience factors. Yet, it can be the most powerful. Practice the following to strengthen self-reflection:

- Pick a time toward the end of the day when you can take 10 minutes to review the day.
    - o It doesn't have to be the exact same time every day. You could decide to take 10 minutes when you leave the office for the day, on the train/bus going home, or before or after dinner.
- Set a reminder on your calendar for every day.
- From the following list pick three or four questions that are the most relevant for you to answer for yourself (you can pick different questions each day or use the same ones each day).
    - o What did I get done today?
        - ▪ How do I feel about what I accomplished today?

- o What was difficult about what I accomplished today?
  - How can I make things less difficult in the future?
- o Who helped me accomplish things today?
  - How can I strengthen that relationship?
- o Is there someone who was hard to work with today?
  - How can I improve that relationship?
- o Looking back over today, does anything disappoint or frustrate me?
  - What and why?
  - How can I avoid similar disappointments or frustrations going forward?
- o What should I stop doing or do less?
- o What should I do more of?
- o What should I do differently?
- o What's the most important thing I learned today
  - How can I apply that going forward?
- o What opportunity did I miss today?
  - How can I seize similar opportunities going forward?
- o Was I in "the zone" at any point today?
  - What was I doing when I was in "the zone"?
  - How can I do more of that?
- Spend 10 to 15 minutes reflecting on the questions you selected.
- It is best to write down your responses.
- When you are finished, review your answers and decide what changes to commit to.
  - o Write the changes down next to the related answer.
- Take two to three minutes to memorize your list of answers and changes.

Tips

- Don't expect to have huge insights each day.
- Your sense of accomplishment and the things you learn will accumulate over time.

- Share your answers to the day's reflection questions with people who support you.

Why and How This Works!

As discussed in Chapter 1, even before the pandemic the amount of data, information, and digital noise coming at us was overwhelming our perceptual and cognitive abilities. We don't perceive as much as 80 percent of the input we receive.

The two major parts of the brain responsible for memory are the hippocampus and the neocortex. The hippocampus is a structure with two halves, one positioned in each of the brain's hemispheres. Figure 35 illustrates the complex anatomy of one half.

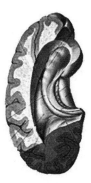

Figure 37: The Hippocampus
Illustration drawn by Dr. Johannes Sobotta. Public Domain

Studies of people whose hippocampus has been bilaterally damaged by disease or injury have led to an understanding of the hippocampus's essential role in memory creation.[52] Without a functioning hippocampus, we lose the ability to learn new facts. Our ability to recall old memories is also somewhat decreased.

During the day facts that you perceive are captured by the hippocampus, which acts as a temporary storage area for the neural connections that are created by the perception of these new facts. Initially, the different neural connections responsible for remembering a fact or set of facts may not be well-organized. As a short-term storage unit, the hippocampus has a limited capacity that can be overwhelmed, in which case new neural networks may overwrite existing ones, and facts and information are lost for good. This is called interference forgetting.[53]

Memory consolidation is a neurologic exchange between the hippocampus and the neocortex. The memories initially dependent on the hippocampus become reorganized into long-term memories primarily stored in the neocortex. The short-term memories are converted to long-term memories by the development of complex, interconnected neural networks distributed across different parts of the neocortex.[54]

When you self-reflect at the end of the day, you are enabling this process. You are sorting through your short-term memories of new information and identifying which of these are useful and important to you.

Also, there is mounting evidence that targeting important short-term memories increases the brain's efficiency in converting them to long-term memory.[55] Following the self-reflection routine may have a similar effect.

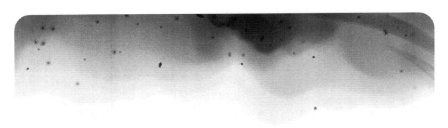

CHAPTER 14

SLEEP: AN ESSENTIAL RESOURCE

llowing ourselves sufficient, high-quality sleep is one of the most powerful things we can do to improve our emotional and physical health and extend our life. If you understand that and recognize you would benefit from sleeping, start using the following routine tonight.

If you're one of the majority of individuals who believe they sleep enough, please see this chapter's section about why and how it works.

The Routine

There are 15 behaviors to practice to improve your sleep:

1. Stick to a sleep schedule of eight hours, beginning and ending the same time each evening.
2. Get outside in the sunlight for a minimum of 30 minutes each day.
   - Do this even on cloudy days.
3. Don't nap after 3 p.m.
4. Finish exercising three hours before it is time for you to sleep.
5. Avoid caffeine in the evening.

- It takes eight hours for the effects of caffeine to diminish completely.

6. Avoid alcohol use in the evening.
7. Avoid heavy meals later in the evening.
8. Talk to your healthcare provider about these questions:
   - Are there any prescribed or over-the-counter medications you are taking that may be interfering with the quality of your sleep?
   - If so, can you take them earlier in the day?
   - Don't change your medications or the times you take them until you have discussed this with your healthcare provider.
9. Keep the bedroom for sleeping.
   - No smartphones or screens of any kind.
   - Keep a slightly cool temperature.
   - Use window coverings that block out streetlights and the early morning sun.
10. Disconnect from screens and technology at least 60 minutes before it is time to sleep.
11. Relax for an hour or so right before sleep time.
12. Take a hot bath right before going to bed.
13. Just before you put your head on your pillow, write down five things that went well (see the gratitude exercise in Chapter 4: Pragmatic Optimism).
14. Practice the body scan meditation as you lie in bed.
15. Don't lie in bed awake.
    - If you are awake for 20 minutes or start to feel anxious about falling asleep, get up and do something relaxing until you feel sleepy again.

Why and How It Works!

You and I are so exhausted we don't even know it. We're confident that despite more than 17,000 studies showing the benefits of eight hours of sleep, we don't need that much. For us, six hours of sleep a night is plenty and, in a pinch, we can get along on five hours.

That's our standard: How little sleep can we get along on? The less sleep we can get along on, the more resilient we must be. Dead wrong. Resilience is the ability to thrive amid adversity.

People who sleep less than six hours a night have a memory deficit of up to 40 percent compared with those who sleep eight hours. So if you sleep six or fewer hours tonight, tomorrow when you wake up you won't remember 40 percent of the information you learned today.[56] That much information will not be hard-wired into your brain.

All of the factors that build your resilience depend on hard-wiring your brain; the last two hours of eight hours of sleep are when the majority of that hard-wiring occurs.

We tend to think about every hour of sleep as having the same benefits. That's simply not true. Sleep is an intricate, highly active, neurologic dance with different moves and benefits throughout the eight hours.

Here's a high-level look at the process of sleeping. There are two types of sleep:

- Non-Rapid Eye Movement (NREM)
- Rapid Eye Movement (REM)

Each type of sleep performs different functions and provides different benefits.

In REM sleep our brain is so active that brain energy, as measured by glucose and oxygen metabolism, equals or exceeds energy use when we are awake. This is why REM sleep is also called paradoxical sleep. There are three primary functions of REM sleep:

- Dreaming
- Memory consolidation in concert with the hippocampus
- Restores brain chemistry to a normal balance

During REM sleep your body is totally limp as if it were paralyzed. It is believed that this evolved to protect us from actually acting out our dreams.

NREM sleep is categorized into four stages from 1 to 4. Stage 1 is the shallowest stage, and stage 4 is the deepest stage. How difficult it is to wake someone from sleep is what is meant by the relative shallowness or depth of each stage.

NREM sleep functions to delete unneeded neural connections. This cleaning out of unnecessary connections, particularly early in the night's sleep, prepares for the consolidation and strengthening of new, important neural connections during REM sleep.

Working hand in hand, NREM and REM sleep play an essential part in rewiring our brain each night based on the previous day's experiences.

Every 90 minutes you go through a sleep cycle of REM and NREM sleep. As you can see in Figure 38, the sequence of each cycle is the same, but the proportions of REM and NREM sleep differ significantly. In cycle 1 you spend the majority of the 90 minutes in the deepest stages of sleep— NREM stage 4—but very little time in REM sleep. Over the course of eight hours of sleep the proportions dramatically shift. By cycle 5 you are spending no time in NREM stages 3 and 4 and the majority of time in REM sleep.

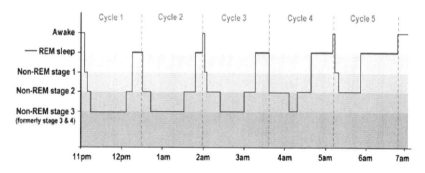

Figure 38: An Eight-Hour Sleep Cycle

When you sleep six hours or less, you deprive your brain of the sleep cycle that performs the most in memory consolidation (i.e., transferring memories from the short-term storage in the hippocampus to the long-term storage in the neocortex). Sleeping 25 percent less than eight hours costs you 60 to 90 percent of your REM sleep.[57] Sleeping six hours or less causes you to experience a deficit of between 20 and 40 percent of the memories stored in the hippocampus the day before.

Up to now, we've been focused on academic or factual learning. What about motor skills learning?

Often when we're learning new motor skills—including playing the piano or using a power tool or playing sports—our initial performance is rough. Often we extend our practice sessions out of frustration at our inability to get smooth and reliable performance. When we do this our frustration increases because our performance actually declines with more practice. If we get eight hours sleep the night following a day of practicing new motor skills, our brain smooths out our performance. It becomes more fluid and consistent. We also get significantly faster at performing new motor skills after a full night's sleep. These benefits directly correlate to the amount of NREM stage 2, particularly in the last two hours of eight hours of sleep.

Another detriment of getting less than six hours of sleep is that we become exhausted 10 to 30 percent faster. In today's environment of tremendous uncertainty and anxiety, our time to exhaustion is already decreased. Losing another 30 percent of our energy can be crippling.

Building your resilience is predicated on the ability to rewire your brain. The most essential parts of that rewiring occur in the final two hours of an eight-hour period of sleep.

Cutting back on sleep can be deadly in the immediate and the short term. Research by the AAA Foundation for Traffic Safety demonstrates the dramatic increase in crashes by drivers who are have as little as two hours of sleep. Postponing sleep can be just as deadly. When you are awake for 19 hours straight, you are as impaired as someone who is legally drunk.

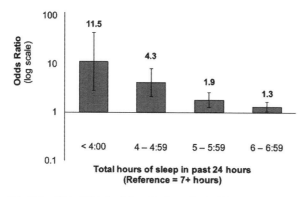

Data: National Motor Vehicle Crash Causation Survey (National Highway Traffic Safety Administration, 2008).

Figure 39: Study Shows Increase of Car Accidents
as Amount of Sleep Declines

The longer-term threats to life include the destruction of your immune system. In the midst of a pandemic an effective immune system may literally be the difference between life and death. Hundreds of studies demonstrate that sleep deprivation doubles your risk of getting cancer. Diabetes and obesity also significantly increase with sleep deprivation. The less you sleep, the more you eat so your body loses the ability to manage your blood sugar.

Sleep deprivation also increases the likelihood of depression and anxiety. Anxiety is the biggest barrier to you, your colleagues, your family, and our society moving forward out of this massive uncertainty into a phase of New Beginnings.

At this moment we are all anxiously awaiting in the midst of the roll-out of COVID-19 vaccines. The vaccines offer the promise of true safety and good health. A vaccine works by triggering the body's process of creating antibodies to defeat the virus when it enters our system. When this works, we have no ill effects and don't spread the deadly infection to others.

Here's the problem: People who get between seven and nine hours of sleep produce a tremendous amount of antibodies. Those who are sleep deprived produce less that 50 percent of the antibodies produced by those who get sufficient sleep. Worse yet, you can't correct the problem by getting more sleep after you receive the vaccine. When the vaccine is available, if you are even minimally sleep deprived, you will have compromised its effectiveness. You will remain at an unnecessary risk of contracting the virus.

By now you may be thinking "this is very troubling...I know I'm not sleep deprived."

That's the real challenge here. When you are chronically sleep deprived, your brain and your body acclimate to the deficit. While you will experience low energy, you will define it as normal, perhaps as a result of work or family pressures, rather than as a result of lack of sleep. And short-term attempts to catch up on lost sleep don't work. Many people go through the entire week sleep deprived and then sleep longer hours on Friday and Saturday nights. This doesn't make up for the damaging effects of sleep deprivation. Only getting eight hours of sleep on a sustained basis can return you to good health.

As Dr. Matthew Walker writes in his book *Why We Sleep: Unlocking the Power of Sleep and Dreams*: "There does not seem to be one major organ within the body, or process within the brain, that isn't optimally enhanced by sleep (and detrimentally impaired when we don't get enough)."

As noted in Chapter 1, our anxiety is fueled by our lack of clarity about the future and control in the present moment. Getting eight hours of sleep gives us the clarity of knowing that by taking control of our sleep we can powerfully enhance our health, increasing our chances of warding off the virus now and getting full benefit of the vaccine in our future.

Thriving amidst uncertainty is dependent on our ability to control the rewiring of our brain, which is largely dependent on consistently sleeping eight hours each night.

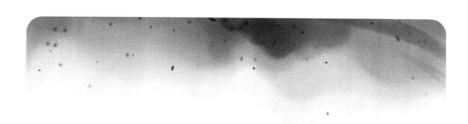

CHAPTER 15

THREE ROUTINES TO MINIMIZE ANXIETY

This chapter provides three routines for you to practice daily to keep your anxiety as low as possible throughout the day:

- Waking up to manage stress: A checklist
- Staying calm during the day
- Winding down to sleep: A checklist

Each routine includes resilience building behaviors described in our earlier chapters, particularly from the following chapters:

- Chapter 4: Pragmatic Optimism
- Chapter 5: Focus
- Chapter 6: Building Empathy

The third checklist on winding down to sleep also includes steps described in Chapter 14: Sleep: An Essential Resource.

All of the techniques included in each checklist are provided for easy reference. For more detailed discussion, see the relevant chapter.

As discussed in Chapter 3: Resilience: The Science of Thriving Amidst Adversity, these are the first three factors you should focus on developing as we journey through Uncertainty into our future of New Beginnings.

Waking Up to Manage Stress: A Checklist

1. Before you rise meditate for three minutes (see meditation guidance below).
2. Wait 20 to 30 minutes before you check emails/texts/social media/news sources.
3. Answer the Pragmatic Optimism questions (see below).
4. Eat breakfast and hydrate with water.
5. Double-check you have all your stuff.
6. Before you enter your workplace (even if working at home), visualize a successful day (see below).

Three-Minute Breathing Meditation

- Touch each of your index fingers to the thumb on the same hand.
- Close your eyes or gaze softly at a point six or so feet away.
- Take a moment to focus on what you are feeling physically.
- Focus on where you are feeling your breathing most clearly: belly, chest, nostrils, or mouth.
- As you breathe in think: "Breathing in, I know I am breathing in."
- As you breathe out, think: "Breathing out, I know I am breathing out."
- When your mind wanders, simply bring your attention back to your breathing.
- Continue for three minutes.

The Pragmatic Optimism Questions

Question: Will this last forever?
Answer: No. Nothing about this situation will last forever. Not the shortage of vital equipment. Not the number of people becoming infected. Not the anxiety and fear.

Question: Will this really impact everything important to me?
Answer: No. When this is over the things that really matter will be there. Some things that are important will be even better.

Question: Today, how can I use my experience and skills to make this just a little bit better?
Your Answer:_____

Repeat these questions and your answers to yourself during the day.

Visualizing A Successful Day

1. Sit quietly.
2. Take a few deep belly breaths.
3. Think of a challenge or goal for today.
4. Close your eyes or gaze softly at a point six feet in front of you.
5. Take your time imagining how you go through the day to achieve success.
6. Imagine what it will look like and feel like when you have succeeded overcoming your challenge or achieving your goal.
7. Do these for three to four minutes.

Staying Calm During the Day

Check the box each time you perform a technique.

- ☐ 1. Use the S.T.O.P. technique—three times (see below).
- ☐ 2. Practice loving kindness—three times (see below).
- ☐ 3. Practice belly breathing for three minutes—three times (see below).
- ☐ 4. Use the Ladder of Inference—one time (see below).
- ☐ 5. Use the BATHE technique—one time (see below).
- ☐ 6. Use the four most powerful questions—one time (see below).

The S.T.O.P. Technique

Whenever you are tempted to give in to a craving, do the following:

1. Stop what you are doing.
2. Take a mindful breath (focus your attention on a slow, deep breath).
3. Observe what you are doing and what you are thinking.
4. Proceed to keep doing what you are doing or give in to the craving.

Loving Kindness

When you are encountering someone who you want to develop an empathetic relationship with, think to yourself in regard to them:

- May you be safe.
- May you be healthy.
- May you be happy.
- May you live with ease.
- May you live with purpose.

Next, think those same things in regard to yourself:

- May I be safe.
- May I be healthy.
- May I be happy.
- May I live with ease.
- May I live with purpose.

Belly Breathing

- Close your eyes or gaze softly at a point six or so feet away.
- Notice how you are breathing.
- Breathe through your nose.

- Put one hand below your belly button.
- Put your other hand at the center of your upper chest.
- Inhale as you expand your belly out and feel your hand rising.
- Exhale and feel your belly go flat—like a balloon flattening.
- Continue for three minutes.

The Ladder of Inference

To use the Ladder of Inference to improve your fact-based decision-making:

- Begin anchoring yourself in the pool of "All The Facts."
  - o Take your time gathering facts.
- When you have as full a set of perceived facts as possible, allow yourself to add assumptions to fill in the missing pieces in the fact puzzle.
- Next, state or write down your conclusions and the actions you would take based upon them.
- Now force yourself to go to the bottom of the ladder to see if you can pull more facts out of the pool and into the set of facts you perceive.
- Once you have an expanded set of facts, go back up the ladder.
- When you get to your assumptions, compare them with the new facts you have gathered.
- Do the new facts contradict or support your assumptions?
- At the conclusion level, ask yourself: Do the new facts and assumptions change my understanding of the situation and the actions called for?

The BATHE Technique

This technique is used to build empathy with another person.

- ☐ Background: How are things?
- ☐ Affect: How do you feel about it?

- [ ] Troubles: What troubles you the most?
- [ ] How are you handling the situation?
- [ ] Empathy: Convey understanding

The Four Most Powerful Questions

- [ ] What do you want?
- [ ] What are you doing?
- [ ] How is that working?
- [ ] What is your plan?

Winding Down to Sleep: A Checklist

There are 15 behaviors to practice to improve your sleep:

- [ ] Stick to a sleep schedule of eight hours, being at the same time each evening.
- [ ] Get outside in the sunlight for a minimum of 30 minutes each day.
  - Do this even on cloudy days.
- [ ] Don't nap after 3 p.m.
- [ ] Finish exercising three hours before it's time for you to sleep.
- [ ] Avoid caffeine in the evening.
  - It takes eight hours for the effects of caffeine to diminish completely.
- [ ] Avoid alcohol use in the evening.
- [ ] Avoid heavy meals later in the evening.
- [ ] Talk to your healthcare provider about these questions:
  - Are there any prescribed or over-the-counter medications you are taking that may be interfering with the quality of your sleep?
  - If so, can you take them earlier in the day?
  - Don't change your medications or the times you take them until you have discussed this with your healthcare provider.

☐ Keep the bedroom for sleeping.
  - No smartphones or screens of any kind.
  - Keep a slightly cool temperature.
  - Use window coverings that block out streetlights and the early morning sun.

☐ Disconnect from screens and technology at least 60 minutes before it's time to sleep.

☐ Relax for an hour or so right before sleep time.

☐ Take a hot bath right before going to bed.

☐ Just before you put your head on your pillow, write down five things that went well (see the gratitude exercise below).

☐ Practice the body scan meditation as you lie in bed.

☐ Don't lie in bed awake.
  - If you are awake for 20 minutes or start to feel anxious about falling asleep, get up and do something relaxing until you feel sleepy again.

The Gratitude Exercise

- Place a pad or small notebook and pen/pencil by your bedside.
- Immediately before lying down to sleep, write down five things that went well that day.

Tips

- They don't have to be "big" things. The fact that you got out for a few minutes to enjoy the sunny day or someone paid you a compliment, or you carried out an act of kindness are all good examples of things that went well.
- Make sure you write these things down on paper, not input them into your smartphone.

CHAPTER 16

USING RESILIENCE TO MOVE THROUGH GRIEF

As we discussed in Chapter 1, a multitude of losses are leaving most, if not all of us, in an ocean of grief—an ocean where riptides seem to suck us out as we try to gain a foothold on some kind of stable emotional shore. Even in the strongest riptide, there are techniques to make it back to shore. The most common is simply to swim parallel to the shore until we are out of the powerful riptide. In this emotional sea of riptides of grief we can rely on resilience techniques to break free of the bonds of grief to move forward. This chapter provides the guidance to do so.

Helping someone navigate through grief requires a series of conversations. I'll provide two checklists to structure the initial conversation and then subsequent conversations. An essential step in successfully helping someone through the grieving process is to spend time emotionally and mentally preparing yourself for each conversation.

Before I get into the checklists, let me share some personal experiences with my grief and the grief of others in the aftermath of disasters. From them I draw seven lessons for grieving. I share these for the same reason so many others have shared their grief with me—to give you hope and help you move forward.

One of the most important things to understand about grief and trauma is "one event, different experiences." Over the years I've met and worked with hundreds of first responders and survivors of the 9/11 attacks. I've never found two people who had the same experience of the same event. The same trauma doesn't impact any two people the same way.

I belong (for lack of a better term) to several communities impacted by disaster and the accompanying losses, which means that to heal they must go through the grieving process. By being part of these communities, I've learned the truth and wisdom of "one event, different experiences."

The community of people who lost loved ones in the April 24, 1997, bombing of the Murrah Building in Oklahoma City has become deeply connected to a community of those of us impacted by the September 11, 2001 attacks in New York City. Since the first anniversary of 9/11, groups from each city have traveled to the other on the anniversary of their attack. Together, the groups learn from each other how to move forward. Most importantly, we learn there is no single path through grief, but there is a path.

In Oklahoma, the blast killed 168 people including 19 children. Among the dead were at least three pregnant women. More than 600 people were injured. My dear friend and brother Jack Poe was Chief of Chaplains for the Oklahoma City Police Department on that day and played a major role in the rescue and recovery. He and his wife, Phyllis, (also a Police Chaplain) still grieve the losses of that day from a place of acceptance.

In March of 2002 I received a phone call from an Associate Pastor of the Council Road Baptist Church in Bethany, OK. After introducing himself, he said: "Jack Poe suggested I call you. And if I might ask you a favor..." I immediately cut him off because I knew "what Jack Poe wants, Jack Poe gets." A bit taken aback, he continued: "Well, in our little church we want to dedicate our Sunday services to remembering the 9/11 attacks. Jack thought you might join us." I interrupted again, "What Jack Poe wants, Jack Poe gets." And so we agreed my wife, Maureen, and I would fly to Oklahoma City on Friday, September 6, 2002, so I could join Jack in the memorial services at "this small church."

Fortunately, my wife, Maureen, who had already endured so much, agreed to the trip.

I wasn't just willing to "do Jack a favor"; I was driven. Why was I driven? Very simply, I was trying to get and stay in the state of acceptance. To do that meant I had to find meaning in the tragic event of 9/11 and my experience of it. Giving back to Jack and his community seemed one clear way of doing that.

As I recall, it was Friday, September 14, 2001, and I was working at Ground Zero next to one of two disaster mortuary tents (DMT). This one was on Vesey Street right outside of the World Financial Center. It was mid-afternoon around 3 p.m. There were no clergy present at the DMT. Over 90 percent of New York firefighters were Catholic at the time. Not having a priest or any clergy present as the remains of their fellow firefighters and civilians who had perished was heartbreaking. I foolishly declared I would go get some clergy. It turns out I wasn't so foolish. I am a man of faith and believe that God intervened on our behalf.

Within half a block I saw a man wearing a yellow hard hat with the word Chaplain printed just above the brim. He was wearing a blue jumpsuit with the badge of the Oklahoma City Police Department embroidered on its upper left chest. This was Jack Poe, Chief of Chaplains, Oklahoma City Police Department, followed by nine more experienced Southern Baptist chaplains from Oklahoma City.

For the next 10 days, they ministered to our needs. Perhaps more importantly, they shared with us what was to come. They each shared and gave strength by sharing their own journeys through grief. They also told us how grief would impact us and all the people in and around New York City.

I remember one day in particular when Jack and I walked around the pile, stopping from time to time to comfort a rescue worker. Along the way Jack quietly explained to me how grief would at first energize and unify us and people from across the country and indeed the world. He spoke quietly about what that felt like for himself and different people after the Murrah Building bombing and how over time that unity would break down as people moved into the various stages of grief. Many people would become stuck in one component or another. Some in denial, some in anger, some in sadness so deep it became despair, some in bargaining, and a few in acceptance. His lessons were, unfortunately, prophetic.

Figure 40: Chaplains and First Responders Reuniting at Ground Zero. On the 5th anniversary of the 9/11 attacks four of the Chaplains from Oklahoma City came to continue to help us heal and strengthen the bonds of two communities who lost so much. Left to Right: Chaplain Paul Bettis; Chief of Chaplains, Jack Poe; MTA Bridge & Tunnel employee Anthony Pisciotta who dug selflessly to recover victims; Chaplain Bob Nigh; Chaplain Sam Porter; and myself.

For me, I immediately recognized I was stuck in bargaining. That's how I prayed to God. "God, if you would only. . ., I promise...." In December I began to show signs of what later would be diagnosed as post-traumatic stress disorder (PTSD). The single greatest emotion I felt at that time was sadness so deep it felt like I was at the bottom of a well. In early 2002 I left my employer Merrill Lynch, having decided to take some time off. Instead, I was offered a position as Global Managing Director for Development of the Sales Force of then Willis Holdings, which had its New York headquarters then at 10 Hanover Plaza, adjacent to Water Street in downtown New York City. Going to and from work required me to pass Ground Zero twice a day.

My grief moved from sadness to anger. Every time I saw tourists gazing into the pit or gathering outside Ten House,[58] I became inflamed.

I wanted to (but, fortunately, never did) punch one of the many tourists trying to get over fences and barriers to take pictures of the recovery operation.

By the time I got the call from the Associate Pastor, I was still battling PTSD; my grief was progressing into acceptance. I needed to do something to add meaning to so much loss—and if speaking at a small church would do that, I was grateful for the opportunity.

Maureen and I arrived in Oklahoma City on Friday night, and Jack and Phyllis Poe met us at the airport and dropped us at our hotel. The next morning they picked us up, and we had a lovely lunch with the pastor of a small church. That evening we shared dinner with Jack and Phyllis and two of the Oklahoma police officers who had come to our aid at Ground Zero.

On Sunday morning, bright and early, Jack and Phyllis picked us up to take us to church. We parked outside of what looked to us like a good-sized community college with a half-dozen or more large buildings. Maureen and I both thought the church must be inside of one of the buildings.

We went through one of six or seven sets of glass doors into the building—and found ourselves immediately in the sanctuary. It was a sanctuary that held 3,000 people like a very large theatre. As we looked in, Maureen and I were awestruck by a huge stage—a stage that held a pulpit, a full orchestra, and a full band. Two large projection screens on either side showed huge pictures of Jack and me. So much for a "small church."

We had agreed with the pastor that he would sit with Jack and me in front of the pulpit and just ask us questions about our experiences. My grief moved from tremendous sadness in anticipation of the first anniversary of the attacks to acceptance—acceptance that it had happened and I needed to move forward. I was here to help people and give meaning to my experience of the events of 9/11.

There were two services, each packed with an overflow crowd in the hallways. Without a word, Jack and I came to the same decision: We would share our experiences and our confidence that we would move forward to help a community that had been grief-stricken by another terrorist bombing some five years earlier. We fully shared our experiences. I shared that my emotional survival of 9/11 was the result of my wife insisting I couldn't return to Ground Zero unless I immediately went into therapy. More than that, Maureen literally took my hand each day to guide me forward. I shared that in January 2002 I began taking Celexa to lessen the sadness, which had moved to depression. I said to the congregation at both services: "Now you should understand I am a middle-aged, white, Irish, Catholic male. We just don't do therapy, and we don't do medication. And if we did, we sure wouldn't talk about it." Each time I got a laugh from the congregation.

After each service Jack and I were surrounded by police officers, firefighters, and EMTs thanking us for sharing. Many said our public sharing gave them permission to finally go get help to move forward through their journey of grief. On future trips to Oklahoma City I met many of those men and women. Happily, they were continuing on their journey.

Since then I've been back to Oklahoma City several times to observe the memorial of the Murrah Building attack, and I've welcomed friends from there who come to New York City on 9/11 to comfort us.

Along the way I met Ken Thompson, son of Virginia Thompson, who was one of the last three victims recovered from the Murrah Building. When I met Ken he worked for the Oklahoma City National Memorial Foundation. Ken had a wife and kids and a career on the day of the bombing. He left the career behind and took time away from his family to help others heal in memory of his mom.

Here's what Ken taught me and thousands of others about grief.

"There is a hole in my heart that is empty. It will never be filled. And that's okay, because that hole in my heart reminds me of how much I love my Mother and always will."—Ken Thompson

Please indulge me with a bit more storytelling before I summarize the lessons I've learned.

On October 24, 2012, Hurricane Sandy hit the eastern coast of the United States. It devastated the coasts of New York and New Jersey. On October 24, 2012, I joined HEART 9/11 in Brooklyn, New York, to help in the recovery. In Chapter 6: Building Empathy, I shared some of my experiences. Let me take a few moments to share the grieving I witnessed.

Perhaps the most compelling version of grief that I witnessed was meeting some of the people who were absolutely driven to keep working on the recovery—around the clock with no break! Some were sanitation workers who worked for New York City. They were driven to clean up the streets of the community of Gerritsen Beach. Others were New York City firefighters and paramedics who did double shifts for months—long after the need to help those impacted by the hurricane itself. Community members worked tirelessly to distribute food and supplies and to organize and run the community's response. I confess for months I was one of those so driven. What part of grief causes such effort? Eventually, it can become debilitating.

I think one or two aspects of grieving cause this. First, anger—including anger at the unfairness of the random storm and its devastation. The second is denial: If we work hard enough, it will be like this never happened, and things will go back to normal.

On December 14, 2012, while in Gerritsen Beach, Brooklyn, I heard of the horrific Sandy Hook school shooting in Newtown,

Connecticut. One week later a woman came to the construction trailer that served as our headquarters in Gerritsen Beach. She was the aunt of one of the children murdered the week before. The young boy's name was Daniel Barden, and he was seven years old. His aunt had brought with her seven brand new bikes—one for each year of Daniel's life. She said to us, "Daniel loved to ride his bike.... I didn't know what else to do....I thought some of the children here could ride for him."

We had a drawing to decide which children would receive the bikes. Hundreds of community members gathered round for the drawing, their eyes filled with tears.

Daniel Barden, Age 7

Encouraged by the compassionate bravery

of Daniel's aunt, the kids riding those bikes around Gerritsen Beach received and gave hope and encouragement for years to come.

Finally, let me share the connection between the Murrah Building bombing and the attacks on the Twin Towers and Hurricane Sandy.

In the aftermath of the Murrah Building bombing, temporary fences were erected around the site. People from the city, around the country, and the world would tie notes, flowers, and pictures to the fence in memory of those who were lost, along with Teddy Bears. Hundreds of Teddy Bears were tied to or placed at the foot of the fencing. Some were tagged with the name of one of the children lost in the attack. Others were just left for those lost.

A few weeks after 9/11, Jack Poe and Chaplain Leslie Sias[59] returned to Ground Zero to continue to minister to us. They were followed by an 18-wheeler jammed with thousands of Teddy Bears sent by the people of Oklahoma City. It took almost two weeks to distribute them. A few hundred went to students with disabilities at New York public schools. The rest? To first responders—firefighters, law enforcement officers, EMTs, and sanitation workers who had held in their pain for weeks took and hugged Teddy Bears. Whether it was the bears themselves, the notes attached, or the connection to another community that knew the pain of loss from a terrorist attack, Teddy Bears opened the path to grieving.

Eleven years later at Gerritsen Beach, I remembered the healing power of Teddy Bears. I reached out to Tom Bowles, CEO of Enesco, the company that manufactures Gund Teddy Bears. I wondered if Enesco could donate a few of the smaller bears for me to distribute to some of the people of Gerritsen Beach. Within a week several thousand brand new bears were delivered. They filled a garage and ranged from the tiniest to the largest. We distributed them to the men, women, and children of Gerritsen Beach. We told them the story of the bears of Oklahoma and of Ground Zero. We asked them to put their bear in a place where they could see it every day. We asked that each day when they looked at it they envision it being in their newly rebuilt home. Once again, Teddy Bears opened the door to the healing that comes from the natural process of grieving.

The story of the healing Teddy Bears is shared with the adults and children of Gerritsen Beach. Each person received their own to begin healing.

Figure 41: Teddy Bears Inviting People to Grieve

What are the lessons of grieving that we can use to aid us as we move through a time of global grieving for so many reasons?

1. The same event/loss is experienced by each of us in a unique way.
2. Grief is a natural and necessary process. Avoiding grief is a sure path to suffering.
3. It's essential to allow yourself to grieve and to be kind to yourself in the process.
4. The memories of what we lost will not disappear. The pain will dull while the love of what has been lost will remain.
5. Sharing our grief gives others permission to make their grief journey and to heal.
6. Shared grief creates bonds of a lifetime that cross geographies, races, religions, ages, and all the other meaningless differences among human beings.
7. Those that have gone before us want to show us the way while learning what our grief experience is.

8. Creating meaning out of grief comes from acceptance of our loss and the need to move forward, making the world in some small way a better place.

9. The path of grieving can be confusing as you shift through different parts from bargaining to anger, sadness, denial, and then to acceptance.

Now let's look at our two checklists for engaging in empathetic and compassionate conversations with someone who is grieving.

Helping Another Navigate Through Grief: Checklist for the Initial Conversation

☐ 1. Practice self-empathy with loving kindness (see below).
☐ 2. Do a breathing meditation (see below).
☐ 3. Arrive mindfully (see below).
☐ 4. Use the BATHE technique (see below).
☐ 5. Take cleansing breaths periodically (see below).
☐ 6. Use silence (see below).
☐ 7. Ask: How can I help?
☐ 8. Set a time for your next conversation.

Loving Kindness

When you are about to talk to someone to help them grieve, think to yourself in regard to them:

- May you be safe.
- May you be healthy.
- May you be happy.
- May you live with ease.
- May you live with purpose.

Next, think those same things in regard to yourself:

- May I be safe.
- May I be healthy.
- May I be happy.
- May I live with ease.
- May I live with purpose

Three-Minute Breathing Meditation

☐ Touch each of your index fingers to the thumb on the same hand.

☐ Close your eyes or gaze softly at a point six or so feet away.

☐ Take a moment to focus on what you are feeling physically.

☐ Focus on where you are feeling your breathing most clearly: belly, chest, nostrils, or mouth.

☐ As you breathe in think: "Breathing in, I know I am breathing in."

☐ As you breathe out think: "Breathing out, I know I am breathing out."

☐ When your mind wanders, simply bring your attention back to your breathing.

☐ Continue for three minutes.

Arrive Mindfully

☐ Before you connect with the person who is grieving, simply pause to sit or stand still without talking for 15 to 30 seconds.

☐ Make a mental note of the transition you are making.

   o I am going to call Jim to discuss his grieving over...

☐ If on video, note what you see and look all around.

☐ Note what you hear:

   o Attend to subtle sounds.

   o Listen to tone of voice and pace of speech.

   o Pay attention to word choice.

The BATHE Technique

This technique is used to enable you to understand what the loss means and feels like to the other person.

☐ Background: What are the things that are going on for you?
☐ Affect: How do you feel about these situations?
☐ Troubles: What troubles you the most?
☐ How are you handling these situation?

The Cleansing Breath

Use this when you or the person you are helping need some help gaining control over your emotions.

☐ 1. Inhale deeply through your nose while expanding your belly.
☐ 2. Exhale through puckered lips.
☐ 3. Let your head drop to your chest as you exhale.
☐ 4. Repeat four or five times.

Using Silence

Often we avoid creating empathy and expressing compassion to those who are grieving because we "don't know what to say" or "what if I say the wrong thing?" Often saying nothing is the most powerful way of expressing your compassion.

☐ 1. Sit quietly.
☐ 2. Be present.
☐ 3. Let them choose to talk or just to sit quietly.

Helping Another Navigate Through Grief: Checklist for Ongoing Conversations

- ☐ 1. Practice self-empathy with loving kindness (see above).
- ☐ 2. Do a breathing meditation (see above).
- ☐ 3. Arrive mindfully (see above).
- ☐ 4. Suggest a breathing meditation (see above).
- ☐ 5. Use the BATHE technique (see above).
- ☐ 6. Use the four most powerful questions (see below).
- ☐ 7.. Use fact-based decision-making (see below).
- ☐ 8.. Create options to move forward (see below).
- ☐ 9. Commit to a plan (see below).
- ☐ 10. Set a time to reconnect (see below).

The Four Most Powerful Questions

The four most powerful questions are used to enable a person to motivate themselves. In the case of supporting someone who is grieving, the opportunity to use these presents itself when the person says something such as "I don't know what to do...." The first of the four questions may be particularly difficult for the person to answer. Patience is key. Allow them to answer at their own pace. Don't push; just pose each question as the previous one is answered. If the person can't answer one of the questions, stop and come back to the questions at a future date.

The four most powerful questions are:

1. What do you want?
2. What are you doing?
3. How is that working?
4. What is your plan?

Fact-Based Decision-Making
The Ladder of Inference

To use the Ladder of Inference to improve the grieving person's fact-based decision-making:

- Begin asking them to consider the pool of "All The Facts."
  - o Encourage them to take their time gathering facts.
- When they have as full a set of perceived facts as possible, ask them to add assumptions to fill in the missing pieces in the fact puzzle.
- Next, ask them to state or write down their conclusions and the actions they may take based upon them.
- Now, having listened to their construction of their situation, you go to the bottom of the ladder to see if you can pull more facts out of the pool and into the set of facts they perceive.

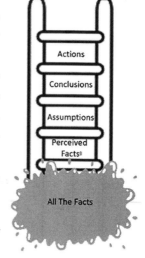

- Now, looking at both the facts you and they perceive, review their assumptions:
  - o Do the new facts you perceive contradict or support some of their assumptions?
  - o Should some of the assumptions be deleted or expanded?
  - o Are there new assumptions that should be added?
- At the conclusion level ask the person: Do the additional facts and assumptions change their understanding of the situation and the choices they have?

Create Options to Move Forward

You can try any of the techniques to create agility, as described in Chapter 8. The one I prefer is aligning options because it keeps what the person wants and all of their options right in front of them.

Aligning Options

By using this technique you hope to show the person they have several choices to move forward, which increases the chances they will continue to move forward when they feel blocked in pursuing a particular solution.

To structure this process, work with the grieving person to complete the worksheet on the next page.

1. State the person's objective.
    *   The objective is generally to move through the grieving process.
    *   A specific objective can be selected by reviewing the person's answers to the first of the four most powerful questions: "What do you want?"
    *   It is best not to ask the person to come up with an objective from scratch so consult that first question and any other objectives the person might have mentioned during your conversations.
    *   In the second row at the top of the worksheet write down the person's objective as clearly and specifically as possible.
2. Determine the criteria.
    *   Across the top you will see boxes labeled Criteria 1 through Criteria 5.
    *   You can have as many as eight criteria.
    *   In each of these boxes write in one specific criteria.
    *   In grieving, some criteria could be:
    *   Become more active.
    *   Reconnect with people.
    *   Give meaning to my loss.
    *   Achieve something useful.
    *   Take a concrete step.
    *   Support my partner/spouse/child in their grieving.
3. Brainstorm options.
    *   The first column on the left is labeled Options.

- Ask the person to come up with as many options as they can without considering their criteria.
4. Evaluate options against the criteria.
    - Once the person has at least eight options, have them evaluate each one against all of their criteria.
5. Select the two or three best options.
    - Have them select the two or three options that best fit their criteria.
6. Choose one of the options to pursue first.
    - Have them pick one option to start moving forward while keeping the other one or two in reserve.
7. When the first option doesn't work, encourage them to go immediately to the second option.

Tips

Suggest the grieving person:

- Be as specific as they can when writing their objective.
- Once they have decided on the criteria against which to evaluate their options, don't change them.
- Evaluate all the options against all the criteria.
    o Don't stop evaluating an option as soon as it doesn't meet a criterion.
- Commit to going with the second option if the first doesn't work and going with the third option if the second doesn't work.
- Notice after evaluating their options that there is almost never a perfect solution.
    o This frees them emotionally to move forward with "less than perfect."

Commit to a Plan

- Keep the plan simple.
- Ask the person to create a list of no more than four or five actions to carry out the option selected.

- Help them to make sure that they will know when each action has been taken or accomplished.
- Keep the timeline for the plan relatively short—no more than two or three weeks.

Set a Time to Reconnect

- Pick a specific time, date, and place (live or virtual) to check in on how they are doing and their progress.
- Reconnect well before the end of the timeline for their plan.
  - o If their plan is to take five actions in two weeks, reconnect in a week.
  - o If you wait until the deadline for the completion of their plan, then you can't help them be successful in meeting it.

CHAPTER 17

THE ROLE OF RESILIENCE IN ELIMINATING RACISM

As discussed in Chapter 3, my meta-model of resilience incorporates 10 different factors to fully develop our resilience. In terms of mitigating anxiety to improve emotional health, physical wellness, and effectiveness in this time of tremendous uncertainty, I have recommended concentrating on a set of three factors: Focus, Pragmatic Optimism, and Empathy.

The emotional, social, legal, and economic complexity of eliminating racism will require each of us to draw on all 10 factors at various times.

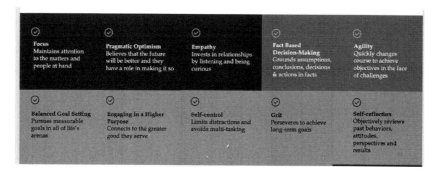

Figure 42: The NResilience Model®

Let me share four perspectives that point to why resilience is an essential part of eliminating racism and how specific resilience factors can help us achieve that goal.

The Challenge of White Fragility

Sociologist and educator Robin DiAngelo describes the concept of White Fragility[60] with these words: "Socialized into a deeply internalized sense of superiority that we either are unaware of or can never admit to ourselves, we become highly fragile in conversations about race. We consider a challenge to our racial worldviews as a challenge to our very identities as good, moral people. Thus, we perceive any attempt to connect us to the system of racism as an unsettling and unfair moral offense."

She goes on to describe our worldview of racism as consisting only of intentional acts by bad people. This view pressures white people to view themselves as immoral and bad people if they admit any involvement in racism.

In truth, racism is a system deeply embedded in our culture, our values, our perceptions, our government and laws, and our way of life.

Unless we understand and accept systemic racism as whites controlling access to civil rights, education, healthcare, and equality, we simply won't see the barriers that prevent the eradication of racism. If we don't see and acknowledge the barriers, we will never remove them.

Systemic racism can only be created by one group having the power to deny another group(s) their human rights. For example, as DiAngelo reminds me, I was taught that women won the right to vote when the 19th Amendment to the Constitution was finally ratified on August 18, 1920. However, state and local laws and regulations continued to keep African American women from voting until the passage of the Voting Rights Act of 1965. The African American woman's right to vote was not realized until white men decided to specifically protect it.

African Americans do not possess the political power to defeat racism. Racism can only be defeated by the collective will and action of white men who hold and wield the power.

Therefore, white men must have the resilience to engage in conversations and actions that challenge their own view of their morality and goodness.

As a white male, the mere title of DiAngelo's book makes me nervous. Reading it forces me to become aware of and accept how I have contributed to racism in my life. It is hard to balance this acceptance with seeing myself as (mostly) a good person.

Here's how resilience factors have helped me to overcome my white fragility.

First, I drew on Focus. I found it essential to stay present as I read about racism and for 10 nights watched documentaries of the civil rights movement and its leaders. The benefits of my meditation practice played a major role in facing racism and its implications for me.

Second, I relied on balanced goal setting and the four most powerful questions, particularly in terms of what I wanted for my family.

What do I want for my children and grandchildren?

I want a more civil, safer, and just world. I want a world with much less violence, injustice, and hate.

What have I been doing?

I've been horrified by the abuses, deaths, and living conditions of African Americans. I haven't been active in eliminating racism. I have been in the fights against school shootings, hunger, and homelessness. I've supported early childhood education, yet I've been a spectator in the 400-year-old struggle for survival and justice of African Americans.

How is that working?

It's not. I'm not contributing to the elimination of racism, which is what I want for my family.

What is your plan?

My plan is to take an active role in the struggle against racism, which includes writing this chapter, challenging myself and my white friends to look at systemic racism and find ways to teach resilience as a resource in the struggle.

I've also designed a resilient community that combines Opportunity Zones and waste-to-energy technology to create African American owned businesses as well as access to good housing, education, and healthcare. I'm promoting the concept to three different communities—so far.

The Need for Nuance

The second point of view I want to share is that of Trevor Noah, host of *The Daily Show* and an African American who grew up in the apartheid of South Africa.

"...Americans are always told that there are only two sides to every story, two sides to every debate, two sides to every argument, I'm vehemently opposed to that idea...if you only have two choices people are always going to make one of two choices which means people are automatically going to be against each other...until the American political system can find a way to represent the nuance that exists within America you are going to create this false impression that there is only racism or not racism."

Trevor Noah
CBS News Sunday Morning
July 12, 2020

Noah makes the point that our way of framing the most complex of problems (i.e., racism) leads only to conflict. At every level of debate in the United States, we pick a side and then set out to defeat the opposition. We show no interest in understanding contrasting points of view. We show no respect for those who disagree with us.

For example, I recently witnessed conversations based on the demands to "defund the police." On one particular occasion a woman was shown carrying a sign that said "Abolish the Police." A friend made the immediate comment: "That's ridiculous." Maybe for a white person it is ridiculous, given that our experience is that police are our protectors.

So how do I take Trevor Noah's advice to understand the nuances and find more than two options? I apply the resilience factor of Empathy. I use Empathy not to understand one perception of an experience but to understand as many different perspectives as I can identify.

For example, what if I am an African American mother who has raised her sons to be extremely careful in how they behave if stopped by the police? What if I am one who has seen drug deals in broad daylight on every corner or who has lost a son to gang violence? What if I am one who has witnessed police assaults on African American men that didn't get recorded on an iPhone? From those lived experiences, I can logically conclude that the police have been largely ineffective in solving the violence that has taken life from my community and family—especially when some police have personally added to that violence.

So maybe for an African American mother, her sons might have a better chance of a good life if no money was spent on policing and that money was put into education, housing, and healthcare in her community.

Noah's point is that the defunding of police is a highly nuanced issue without a simple answer. To solve it requires respect, a curiosity about other peoples' points of view, and a tolerance for constructive criticism of our own ideas. Defunding police is a prime example of what Noah is calling out. We frame the issues as having only two sides. There is, at least, another side. Those in power could continue to fund the police in order to select the best, train them well, pay them well, and hold them accountable. Most importantly, they could fund better education, healthcare (including mental health), and housing independently of how much we spend on police.

A number of years ago I was attending a conference in New York City on mental health disparities. One of the speakers was a congressman from the Bronx, New York. I, unfortunately, don't recall his name. What I do remember were his words: "At this point, in addition to the lives lost we have spent billions and billions in Afghanistan and Iraq. The amount spent is equal to just over $1 billion dollars for every congressional district in the United States. Do you know what we could do in the Bronx with a billion dollars?"

My resilience has helped me struggle to find and articulate the nuance. First, I relied on Empathy. I used Empathy to imagine why an African American mother might want to abolish the police. I use Empathy to develop an understanding of what my African American friends have experienced and how those experiences have impacted them. I also use Empathy to understand white people. Today on Facebook an old neighbor insisted there is no such thing as "white advantage." We both grew up in middle-class neighborhoods, went to good schools, and never experienced a day of hunger. I still am trying to understand where his belief is coming from and why he feels the need to express it.

Most importantly, I rely on Fact-Based Decision-Making. How do the people on different sides of an issue select certain facts to build their reality? If I combine all those facts and the related assumptions, I come to different conclusions and potential decisions. The difference in the facts that underlie their decision-making spotlights the nuances of the issue.

The third perspective I want to share is that of Rob Corcoran. Full disclosure: Rob and his wife, Susan, are my daughter Kate's in-laws. Rob was the National Director of Initiatives of Change and the founder of Hope in the Cities. Rob and Susan moved to Richmond, Virginia, in 1980 and devoted most of the next four decades in establishing honest conversations to reduce racism in Virginia as well as communities across the United States and around the globe. In his book *Trustbuilding*,[61] Rob traces the journey of Richmond, Virginia, from a place of racism deeply rooted in the past to a community making significant progress toward healing, reconciliation, and becoming a just and equitable community.

The lessons are simple and striking. First, everything starts with building a foundation of trust. For the Corcoran family, establishing trust meant choosing to live in an integrated community and sending their sons to public schools. That is how they took the first of four steps for having honest conversations: "1. Begin with yourselves...we must model the change we expect of others....need an inner source... to maintain perspective and equilibrium when the going gets tough."

To fulfill this step, I have engaged the Self-Reflection factor. What am I learning about myself as I learn more about racism? What are the ways I can model the world I want for my children and grandchildren? What am I allowing to get in my way?

The second step is to include everyone. As Rob says: "Living as trustbuilders means going toward those whose worldview is different from our own and who challenge our assumptions, people who irritate us, even people whose very presence threatens our sense of comfort and security."[62]

Again, I employ Empathy not only to understand how African Americans have been impacted by their experiences but to understand my white friends who sometimes seem unable to see systemic racism. In this regard, Empathy keeps me from judging them and helps me maintain my own humility.

The third step is to acknowledge history. The people of Richmond did this by "walking through history," which was a "two-mile walk to mark sites previously too painful or shameful to remember." The walk was for people to acknowledge their shared history. The first of these walks was held in 1993 with 500 members from across Richmond's communities as well as people from across the United States and around the globe to offer their support and share their own healing.

As I write this, across the United States offensive statues are being torn down. Sports teams are being renamed, and the Confederate flag was removed from the last state flag to incorporate it. I hope these changes are not occurring so quickly that we are losing the opportunity to understand why and what it was like to be offended by these symbols. If we are moving quickly, we may be again avoiding the truth rather than moving forward.

To acknowledge history and to understand how long a journey this may still be, I rely on Pragmatic Optimism—the belief that things will get better and, in part, because of the decisions and actions I take each day. Will racism last forever? No. Despite being tremendously painful and costly, some progress—not enough—has been made. Is racism going to affect everything that is important? In this case, probably yes. However, many of the things that you and I hold important will get significantly better. How can I use my experiences and talents to address racism? In all the many ways I have used them to address challenges throughout my life.

The fourth step is to build a team—one that includes everyone and where each person commits to being personally responsible for having honest conversations and moving forward.

One of the major breakthroughs came after the statue of the late Arthur Ashe was placed on Monument Avenue, previously reserved only for Confederate monuments. That, combined with the "walking through history", moved honest conversations from the purview of advocates to include the broader community.

"With the polite silence broken, Richmonders felt liberated to enter into honest conversation...”[63]

Another important lesson from Hope in the Cities is that they do not advocate for any position or solution on any issue.

"People ask why we don't do traditional advocacy; I say it's because we intend to be effective. You have to respect the things that people have to do for themselves and their institutions. Otherwise you won't get the change you want."

—*Ben Campbell, Hope in the Cities*[64]

For me, building a team requires engaging in a higher purpose. As Rob describes, at first the higher purpose of racial justice and equality attracts a few early adopters, then a core of advocates and activists forms, and finally the majority of the community engages in achieving that higher purpose.

My own point of view is informed by those above. My point of view is that to eliminate systemic racism we need to pass through the following phases:

1. Acknowledge the truth.

As DiAngelo makes clear in her book, the white majority has to acknowledge that systemic racism not only exists but it's pervasive. Furthermore, while anyone of any race can take racist actions toward another, only those in power can create and protect systemic racism.

To do this requires drawing on Focus, Balanced Goal-Setting, and Self-control. Together, they allow us to stay present, become motivated, and avoid an "amygdala hijacking" in losing control to our emotions.

2. Stop the bleeding.

I mean this both literally and figuratively. George Floyd was murdered 54 days ago. Since that time there has been a steady stream of reports and videos of police officers physically abusing protestors of all races. There have also been reports and videos of violent protestors assaulting police. We have to stem the flow of blood. Figuratively, the bleeding also continues. For example, the Black Lives Matter mural painted on New York City's Fifth Avenue has been vandalized twice in the past week.

What I see now is a painful reminder of the aftermath of 9/11. At first the attacks united Americans—regardless of race, sexual orientation, economic status, or any other divider. That unity spread around the world. Then, over time, that tremendous power of unity waned.

We need to build our grit to persevere until we achieve what we set out together. We need to engage and partner with the protestors and police officers who joined arms and hearts in the aftermath of George Floyd's murders. We need to develop our Pragmatic Optimism—the belief that things will continue to get better, in part, because of the things we do each day.

3. Have honest conversations.

It's become a "best practice" for corporations and other organizations to establish Employee Resource Groups (ERGs), which are focused on minority groups who suffer from discrimination in the workplace. Usually this includes an African American ERG. A group of African Americans who have suffered from systemic racism in the workplace are tasked with identifying racist policies, procedures, practices, and cultural norms. Best case scenario: Senior management listens, learns, and acts. This is a far cry from embedding the elimination of systemic racism and all other kinds of discrimination into the business' strategy, systems, and processes. ERGs, in fact, make African Americans, who are the victims of racism, responsible for eliminating racism. In the words of a Resident asked to serve on the African American ERG at one major medical center where I consult: "So I lived in a neighborhood where drugs and violence just were. I went to under-funded public schools. We lived in public housing that was uninhabitable. I had to work to overcome all that. All the way through school, I had to work harder and do better than white kids. Now I'm a Resident facing racism here while I focus on becoming an academic physician. And you think I should carry the extra weight of solving a problem that I didn't create...."

ERGs are not bad; they are incomplete. They do not create honest conversations as described by Rob Corcoran between African

Americans and the white majority. They do not foster the consideration of nuance in these discussions called for by Noah Trevor. They place the burden of eliminating racism on those hurt by it.

We need to move past this to where we provide mechanisms for people of all races to have honest conversations so we can build genuine understanding and joint ownership of the solutions.

To achieve this, white leaders of organizations must personally draw on engaging in their higher purpose, practice empathy, and combine fact-based decision-making and agility to bring social justice to the core of the strategy.

4. Invest.

When we—the United States—want to, we spend money in massive amounts. Often this is driven by the belief that something threatens our nation's security. For example, since 2001 we have spent an estimated $5.9 trillion fighting in Iraq and Afghanistan.[65] Putting aside the debate over whether this was wise, effective, or moral, my point is that when the federal government saw a threat to our security, the money flowed.

A second example is when, in the wake of the Great Recession that began in 2008, the federal government spent $498 billion—or 3.5 percent of the GDP—to bail out banks and other financial institutions.[66] Again, my point is not whether this was right or wrong, effective or ineffective. My point is when we saw and acknowledged a threat to our nation, we spent a massive amount of money.

We do not acknowledge the threat to our nation of racism and the related disparities in healthcare, education, housing, employment, and incarceration.

A 2019 report by McKinsey & Co.[67] showed the impact on the US GDP in decreasing the racial wealth gap between now and 2028. Our US GDP would increase by as much as six percent or $1.5 trillion, which amounts to $4,300 per capita and would benefit everyone!

According to a recent report by the Kaiser Family Foundation,[68] healthcare disparities cost an extra $95 billion in increased medical costs and $42 billion in lost productivity, which amounts to $359 per capita.

The total cost of incarcerating prisoners in the United States has often been quoted at approximately $80 billion. A 2017 report found the actual total costs of incarcerating prisoners, including such expenses as judicial costs, was $182 billion.[69] The United States has the highest rate of incarceration of any country on the globe. Let's compare the percentage of the US population versus the percentage of those incarcerated for whites, African Americans, and Hispanics.

While whites equal 63 percent of the US population, they equal only 30 percent of those who are incarcerated. In contrast, African Americans equal only 12 percent of the population but 33 per-cent of those who are incarcerated. For Hispanics, these percentages are 16 percent and 23 percent, respectively.

What if we reduced the ratio of African Americans and Hispanics to the same as whites, (i.e., 47.6 percent)? Almost a million people would not be incarcerated, which is a savings of $78 billion or $203 per person in the United States.

Investing to eliminate only these areas of racial disparity—racial wealth gap, healthcare, and incarcerations—would create a combination of annual economic growth and savings of $1.713 trillion or $4,484 per capita, which, for a family of four, equals $17,937 per year.

To drive investment, we must employ Fact-Based Decision-Making to make the benefits of racial justice clear and tangible. We must use Agility to find ways of making and sustaining the investments that will reduce disparities and create economic and social growth for all.

5. Heal the trauma.

Living in a world where you constantly feel the threat of injury or death often causes psychological trauma. Once we have achieved racial justice and fairness, the trauma experienced by people will not just disappear. It will require healing. For African Americans, the reality of life in a neighborhood where drive-by shootings and drug deaths are all too common is traumatizing. The constant fear of abuse or death at the hands of police is traumatizing, even for African Americans who are living in safe neighborhoods.

Police also suffer from trauma as a result of their work.[70] For po-lice officers, the rates of PTSD and depression are five times greater than those for the general public. The suicide rate for police has been reported as high as 17 per 100,000 versus a national rate of 13 per 100,000. Trauma impairs a police officer's ability to function in the job:

"Police...under stress find it harder than people not experiencing stress to connect with others and regulate their own emotions. They experience narrowed perception, increased anxiety and fearfulness, and degraded cognitive abilities. This can be part of a healthy fight-or-flight response, but it can also lead to significantly greater probabilities of errors in judgment, compromised performance, and injuries. Failing to address the mental health and wellness of officers can ultimately undermine community support for law enforcement and result in officers being less safe on the job."[71]

Developing resilience can help prevent trauma and can help you move forward while suffering from it. However, healing from trauma requires specialized treatment for healing to occur. African Americans and police officers, both of whom have high levels of trauma, need help now and will continue to need it after racial justice is achieved. If not, the impacts of their trauma will impact generations to come.

When dealing with trauma, its survivors, and its healing, I rely on the following factors: Focus, which make it possible for me to stay present in the moment without being distracted by the future and its potential suffering; Empathy, of course, is critical because the same experience traumatizes different people in so many different ways; Fact-Based Decision-Making makes sure I rely on science and educate others to do so as well; and finally, Agility, which allows me to find unique ways to apply the science of healing trauma to the person's individual experience of trauma.

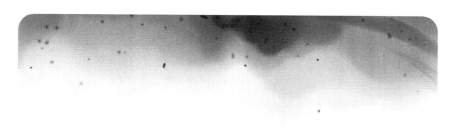

CHAPTER 18

CONCLUSION

Writing this book amidst the pandemic and all the ensuing crises has been a challenge to continually update the facts and events included in it. Today the U.S. is gripped in two epic winter storms. A few minutes ago the temperature in Dallas, Texas was reported at -1^0. Tornadoes, power outages, massive traffic accidents on slippery roads are being experienced in over 30 states.

This past weekend the U.S. Senate acquitted the former President of charges of inciting the January 6th insurrection. After the vote, the Senate Minority Leader – who voted to acquit – read a lengthy statement attesting to the fact that the evidence presented against the former President was accurate and to be believed.

> *"There is no question that President Trump is practically and morally responsible for provoking the events of that day."*
>
> Mitch McConnell
> U.S. Senator from Tennessee
> Senate Minority Leader
> February 13, 2021

So new disasters continue to emerge and the divisiveness in the U.S. continues.

The science and behaviors presented in this book are needed now more than ever. I urge you to practice the behaviors until they became your automatic responses to stress.

Despite all I have witnessed, I remain optimistic. In writing this book I had the time to reflect on the literally hundreds of people who have helped me shape my life and have themselves helped so many people.

The Jana Marie Foundation was founded by Marisa Vicere the young sister of Jana Marie Vicere who lost her life to suicide. JMF continues to fight the stigma of mental illness, to educate young women how to stay healthy and productive, and for communities to have honest conversations about mental health and emotional well-being. JMF's work continues to expand greatly and to save lives.

The Children's Learning Centers of Fairfield County under the leadership of my dear friend Marc Jaffe has stayed open and caring for almost 1,200 children since the beginning of the pandemic. CLC's staff are among the many unsung heros of our time – always serving children with deep commitment for little pay, and over the past year risking their own health so children can keep developing and parents can go to work.

Tuesday's Children, led by my friend and colleague Terry Sears, is expanding its services to help survivors of trauma heal to reach those who have lost someone to COViD. Terry and her team are another group of people who have shown the ability to thrive amidst adversity to serve others.

Levo International continues to embed low-cost, highly efficient hydroponic growing units in Haiti and food desserts in the U.S. My good friend Bill Heiden is the Executive Director who put aside his career to make Levo's vision come to life. A vision created and pursued by Levo's Founder, Bill's son, Christian. Christian saw the vision for Levo when he was still in high school pursuing his Eagle scout badge. Christian is still a college student, yet he has already made an amazing contribution to the hungry people in our world.

In the early months of the pandemic all four of these organizations, JMF, CLC, TC and Levo thought they wouldn't survive the pandemic and the economic crisis. Instead, each one of them chose to thrive amidst chaos. In the midst of all the tragedy we have experienced they continued to make the world a better place.

Yesterday I learned of Proud Puffs, an innovative food product for Black and brown children. Nic King left his corporate job to spend time with his son ended up founding Proud Puffs. Here's what Nic King says about Proud Puffs on his crowd funding site:

"The Proud Puff box was designed to uplift the black and brown community showing the world that representation matters. The characters on the box are my family (Sisters, Nieces, Nephews, and my Son) which ties into my company being called Legacy Cereal. On the side of the box we list 20 influential figures that helped push the culture forward and on the back of the box is an affirmation word search so kids can learn to speak positively about themselves."

Amidst chaos, Nic found a way to move kids away from unhealthy food choices, build their self-confidence, and educate them all at the same time.

So, let me end by practicing what I preach:

Will this last forever?

No. Without doubt the virus will be beaten, the economy will recover. And based on the examples above, we will create a more just and healthier world.

Will I lose everything?

Like everyone I've experienced a lot of personal loss since COViD infected the world. I've also received many blessings personally and professionally. Blessings that will enrich my life well beyond this time of crisis.

How can I use my talents to make a difference?

Lots of ways big and small. Let me invite you to make a difference. Visit the websites of each of the above organizations. You can volunteer, make a donation, or just send them a thank you for what they have brought to our world. All the websites are below.

The Jana Marie Foundation
https://janamariefoundation.org/

The Children's Learning Center of Fairfield County
https://clcfc.org/

Tuesday's Children
https://www.tuesdayschildren.org/

Levo International
https://levointernational.org/

Proud Puffs
https://www.fundblackfounders.com/ProudPuffCereal

Let's each make the world a little better every day.

ABOUT THE AUTHOR

L eo F. Flanagan, Jr., PhD is Founder & President of The Center For Resilience, LLC (CFR). CFR assesses and develops resilience in leaders, employees, teams, organizations and communities. For Leo and CFR resilience is the ability to ***thrive while succeeding***. Currently, he is focusing his consulting efforts with businesses, medical centers, and government agencies on mitigating the anxiety created by COViD-19 and the related economic disruption. Unchecked, anxiety levels will be the major barrier to reducing COViD-19 cases and re-starting our economies and communities.

He is also co-author of a series of online, on-demand classes that develop resilience and stress mitigation skills in people, businesses, and communities at scale. His work is based on the latest neuroscience as well as his leadership experience in responding to disasters from mass suicides to natural disasters to terrorist attacks to school shootings and industrial accidents.

Leo has 30 years of experience in the crafting and activation of human capital strategies. He has guided the assessment and transfor-mation of HR organizations for top global companies such as IBM and McDonald's as well as companies in the $50 to 100M range to fuel profitable growth. He has held senior level corporate HR positions at Merrill Lynch, Willis Holdings, and The Forum Corporation. At Merrill he was responsible for the CEO succession process, assessment, and development of the top 500 leaders and scenario planning for the Board. At Willis he was responsible for the development of the

8,500-person global sales force. He consults across a wide range of industries including digital media, consumer goods, financial services, hospitality, healthcare, manufacturing, and technology.

His brand of Human Resources transformation is fast, lean, practical and integrated with—not burdened on—the business. His work produces a true ROI. Double digit increases in revenue, customer loyalty and employee engagement and reductions in cost are trademarks of his leadership. One leading company recently calculated the ROI from his work at 67:1.

Early in his career, Leo was a faculty member at Cornell University's, School of Industrial and Labor Relations. A regular speaker at leading universities, Carnegie Mellon recently selected him as a faculty member and executive coach for its new The African-American Leadership Institute. The Institute prepares high-potential African Americans for advancement.

Always active in philanthropy and volunteer work, Leo currently is on the Board of Tuesday's Children, an advisor to Children's Learning Centers of Fairfield County and a member of Ministry to the Homeless. As Director of Community Resilience & Behavioral Health for H.E.A.R.T. 911 he volunteered in response to the Newtown School Shooting, Superstorm Sandy and the Moore Oklahoma EF-5 tornado.

Leo earned his PhD at City University of New York, his M.A. at Hunter College and his B.A. at Fordham University. Leo and his wife Maureen have four daughters. They also share a passion for travel as well as skiing, tennis, and sailing. Leo is also an avid fisherman.

ACKNOWLEDGEMENTS

This book is a culmination of my journey beginning in high school. I have been blessed by the mentoring, coaching, and support of many people along the way. The journey started when the late Frank Pandolfo teacher of tenth grade biology challenged a failing student to go speak to the school social workers about volunteering for a hotline. He promised an extra 10 points on my final exam if I just had a conversation. That was my introduction to the world of psychology and helping people overcome crisis and trauma. The late Dr. Michael R. Dattero and his wife Camille Dattero gave me my first lessons in compassion, leadership and serving my community.

The late Andrew (Drew) J. Zambelli, Jr., PhD was a neuropsychologist by training and while still on the faculty of Mercy College had become a force for good in government and community. Drew was only 29 when we met yet he shared an incredible amount of wisdom with me. He gave me my first adjunct faculty appointment at Mercy, and hired me to work on political polling and campaigns. He was a great mentor, teacher and dear friend.

Two weeks into my first semester at the Graduate Center of The City University of New York, the late Professor Morton Bard said "Leo it is not so interesting that people have difficulties in life and need help. What is really interesting is the people who have tremendous difficulties and thrive without help." That brief conversation ignited my passion for resilience.

Professor Suzanne Ouellette-Kobasa who had done the seminal research on hardiness became my very patient, mentor. She introduced me to Dr. Stephen A. Paget at the Hospital for Special Surgery, Steve sponsored my research on hardiness as predictor of outcomes from Total Hip Replacements. He also gave me opportunities to collaborate on several research grants.

Jonathan Rosin for more than 20 years has told me straight when I was off course. He was also the first person, other than family, to reach out to me after 9/11.

Chief of Chaplains, Oklahoma City Police Jack Poe (retired) and the other Chaplains he brought to Ground Zero, including his wife Phyllis, Sam Porter, Leslie Sias, Bob Nigh, and Paul Bettis gave me the benefit of all their experience and compassion initially tested in the horror of the bombing of the Murrah Building in Oklahoma, City. Jack has been my source of spiritual strength and wise counsel for how to help others become resilient in the face of tragedy. Jack, my brother, thanks for being with me the many times we met on the Jericho Road.

The people of Gerritsen Beach, Brooklyn, NY allowed me the privilege of helping them recover from the ravages of Hurricane Sandy. The first intervention to build resilience at scale was delivered in the Gerritsen Beach Volunteer Fire House. In particular, I thank the leaders of Gerritsen Beach Cares and my treasured friends John and Mary Douglas and Jameson Wells.

Al Vicere, Executive Education Professor of Strategic Leadership for the Smeal College of Business at Penn State invited me to join the faculty of the Penn State Hershey Leadership Academy for Excellence in Academic Medicine. This led to an on-going partnership with Dr. Jeffrey Miller, Associate Dean for Administration; Chair, Department of Dermatology, Penn State Health Milton S. Hershey Medical Center and Penn State College of Medicine. Jeff and his colleagues have led the way in discovering how to build resilience within a major academic medical system. I owe a debt of gratitude to Jeff and all his colleagues at Hershey Medical.

Al Vicere also introduced me to his daughter Marisa Vicere. Marisa is the Founder and President of the Jana Marie Foundation (JMF). Marisa founded JMF to promote mental well-being among young people, their families and communities. Marisa founded JMF in memory of her sister Jana Marie who died by suicide. Marisa has partnered with me to create resilience building programs for young people which JMF now delivers across Pennsylvania. The Vicere family are trusted friends who have taught me much about resilience in the face of terrible loss.

Whit Raymond has been a mentor, guide and coach since we first met at Merrill Lynch in 2000. He has read earlier drafts of this book and informed it with insight. Consistently Whit has gifted me with his knowledge of neuroscience and human behavior as well as his own wisdom during my journey.

My dear friend, Dick Dunsing began mentoring and guiding me with his wisdom as we enjoyed a cold beer at a conference in Tampa, FL in 1987. He remains a profound influence on my personal and professional life. Among his many pearls of wisdom "Sit lightly in the saddle, the horse knows the way!"

Kenneth R. Lay has been my friend for more than 30 years and has become my Managing Partner at The Center For Resilience, LLC. With his skill, expertise and compassion we are helping thousands develop their resilience across the globe.

Doug Garr taught me how to do the hard work of writing and how to live a resilient life in the face of on-going hardship.

Frank Troise my spiritual guide who has taught me so much about mindfulness, acceptance and kindness

My son-in-law Andrew Corcoran spent countless hours editing and critiquing my manuscript. He vastly improved this work – and did so while balancing his first child Lizzie on his lap. Andrew's wife Kate and her three sisters, Christina, Lauren and Danielle as well as her Mom, my wife Maureen, made great personal sacrifices while I went off to volunteer at disasters and to serve those in need. Son-in-law Justin and future son-in-law Eddie have added to my blessings.

My mom, Betty Flanagan, now 102, taught me just before her 100th birthday "Don't take sh★t from anyone." She has been a beacon of resilience and of deep religious faith throughout my life.

My sisters Rita and Maureen, brother-in-laws Dom and Tom have been there many times in many ways as have my nephews Tom, Brian, Dom and niece Lisa.

Most importantly I want to acknowledge our youngest generation. My grandchildren Mackenzie, Dillon and Lizzie. My grandnephews Sean, Brian and Monty and my grandnieces Caera, Meghan and Kate. You bring joy, optimism for the future, and purpose to our lives. You've lost much in your young lives. Yet, always look forward as you have taught us to do. Keep in mind the following words:

> *"Every generation, if it is lucky, is called upon to make enormous sacrifices and serve a greater purpose. Meeting the many challenges of the coronavirus pandemic is just such a calling. So, I say to young people, embrace the challenge. Stay strong, stay vigilant, stay positive. Take care of yourself and find ways to help your family and your community. Find ways to help the world emerge as a better place than you found it."*
>
> Philip Ozuah, M.D., Ph.D.
> *CEO*
> *Montefiore Health System*

And finally, to the Holy Spirit who has been my shepherd along my journey.

FOOTNOTES

1   Brennan, Margaret. Interview with President's Chief Medical Advisor Dr. Anthony Fauce: **"Fauci says goal of 100 million coronavirus shots by April "is a floor, not a ceiling".** CBS News: Face The Nation. January 24, 2021. Broadcast

2   Worland, Justin. The soaring twenties. Time Magazine, February 1, 2021

3   Depression and Other Common Mental Disorders: Global Health Estimates. Geneva: World Health Organization; 2017

4   Salari, Nader, et al.. Prevalence of stress, anxiety, depression among general population during COViD-19 Pandemic: A systematic review and meta-analysis. Global Health; 16(1):57 2020 07 06

5   https://www.brainyquote.com/authors/michael-merzenich-quotes.

6   The supportive deferral was taught to me by Stephen Brown who leads development of branch managers and financial advisors for UBS. Thank you, Steve!

7   Hölzel, B.K., Carmody, J., et al. (2011). "Mindfulness Practice Leads to Increases in Regional Brain Gray Matter Density." *Psychiatry Research: Neuroimaging*, 191(1).

8   Williams, M., Teasdale, J., Segal, Z., & Kabat-Zinn, J. (2007). *The Mindful Way Through Depression: Freeing Yourself From Chronic Unhappiness.* The Guildford Press, New York, NY.

9   Killingsworth, M.A., & Gilbert, D.T. (2010). "A Wandering Mind Is an Unhappy Mind." *Science,* 330: 932.

10 Frankel, V.E. (1972). *Man's Search for Meaning: An Introduction to Logotherapy.* Beacon Press.

11 Perry-Smith, B.J., & Bachrach, D.G. (2010). "The Perception of Difficulty in Project-work Planning and Its Impact on Resource Sharing." *Journal Of Operations Management.*

12 Bradberry, T. (10/8/2014). "Multitasking Damages Your Brain and Career, New Studies Suggest." *Forbes*.

13 Damasio, A.R. (2012). *Self Comes To Mind*. Vintage Publishing.

14 Perry-Smith, B.J., & Bachrach, D.G. (2010). "The Perception of Difficulty in Project-work Planning and Its Impact on Resource Sharing." *Journal Of Operations Management*.

15 Coplin, D. (2014). *The Rise of the Humans: How to Outsmart the Digital Deluge*. Harriman House, NY.

16 Evans, L. (9/15/2014). "The Exact Amount of Time You Should Work Every Day: New Research Reveals Exactly How Much Downtime You Should Be Taking." *Fast Company*.

17 Johnson, S., Blanchard, K., et al. (1998). *Who Moved My Cheese?: An A-Mazing Way to Deal with Change in Your Work and in Your Life*. G.P. Putnam and Sons, NY.

18 www.MarionStuart.com.

19 Pennebaker, J. W. (2011). *The Secret Life of Pronouns: What Our Words Say About Us*. Bloomsbury Press. New York.

20 Since the attacks on 9/11, members of Local 79 have been the core of HEART 911's response efforts, as have members of the Carpenters and Ironworkers Unions, among others. They have helped people recover from Gerritsen Beach to New Orleans to Puerto Rico to Haiti. Originally, their efforts were driven by people who had worked at Ground Zero wanting to make greater meaning out of that terrible experience. Now in 2020 some of the Union members who courageously volunteer weren't yet born on 9/11. Their efforts give me great hope.

21 Bennett, M.J. (1979). "Overcoming the Golden Rule: Sympathy and Empathy," *Annals of the International Communication Association*, 3(1): 407-422. doi:10.1080/23808985.1979.11923774.

22 Leung, M.K., Chan, C.C., Yin, J., Lee, C.F., So, K.F., & Lee, T.M. "Increased Gray Matter Volume in the Right Angular and Posterior Parahippocampal Gyri in Loving-Kindness Meditators." *Soc Cogn Affect Neurosci*. 2013;8(1):34-39. doi:10.1093/scan/nss076.

23 Kang, Y., Gray, J.R., & Dovidio, J.F. "The Nondiscriminating Heart: Lovingkindness Meditation Training Decreases Implicit Intergroup Bias." *J Exp Psychol Gen*. 2014;143(3): 1306-1313. doi:10.1037/a0034150.

24 For a discussion of this, see Alter, A. L. (2017*). Irresistible: The Rise of Addictive Technology and the Business of Keeping Us Kooked*. Penguin Press, New York.

25 Brown, B. (2012). *Daring Greatly: How the Courage to Be Vulnerable Transforms the Way We Live, Love, Parent, and Lead*. Avery

26 Bahadur, W., Aziz, S., & Zulfiqar, S. (2018). "Effect of Employee Empathy on Customer Satisfaction and Loyalty During Employee–Customer Interactions: The Mediating Role of Customer Affective Commitment and Perceived

Service Quality." *Cogent Business & Management*, 5(1): 1491780. https://doi. org/10.1080/23311975.2018.1491780.

27 Businesssolver, Inc. (2018). "State of Workplace Empathy Study." Businesssolver.com, Inc.

28 This technique is adapted from Mitroff, I., & Emshoff, J. (1979). "On Strategic Assumption-Making: A Dialectical Approach to Policy and Planning." *Academy of Management Review*, 4(1).

29 Adapted from Senge, P., Kleiner, A., Roberts, C., Ross, R., & Smith, B. (1994). *The Fifth Discipline Fieldbook: Strategies and Tools for Building a Learning Organization.* Pages 385-391. New York, NY: Currency and Doubleday, New York, NY.

30 Adapted from Kahneman, D. (2011). *Thinking Fast and Thinking Slow.* Farrar, Straus, & Giroux.

31 Downloaded from https://upload.wikimedia.org/wikipedia/commons/ thumb/6/65/Cognitive_bias _codex_en.svg/1024px-Cognitive_bias_ codex_en.svg.png.

32 Howard, J., Huang, A., Li, Z., Tufekci, Z., Zdimal, V., van der Westhuizen, H., von Delft, A., Price, A., Fridman, L., Tang, L., Tang, V., Watson, G.L., Bax, C.E., Shaikh, R., Questier, F., Hernandez, D., Chu, L.F., Ramirez, C.M., & Rimoin, A.W. (2020). "Face Masks Against COVID-19: An Evidence Review." *Preprints 2020*, 2020040203 (doi: 10.20944/preprints202004.0203.v1).

33 Davis, C.G., & Asliturk, E. (2011). "Toward a Positive Psychology of Coping With Anticipated Events." *Canadian Psychology*.

34 Mattimore, B.W. (2021). *Idea Stormers: How to Lead and Inspire CREATIVE BREAKTHROUGHS.* Jossey Bass, New York, NY.

35 Kahn, W.A. (1990). "Psychological Conditions of Personal Engagement and Disengagement at Work." *Academy of Management Journal*, 33(4): 692-724.

36 Gallup Corporation. (2017). "State of the American Workplace." Gallup, Inc.

37 Festinger, L. (1962). "Cognitive Dissonance." *Scientific American,* 207(4): 93-106. Retrieved July 3, 2020, from www.jstor.org/stable/24936719.

38 Wortmann, C. (2006). *What's Your Story? Using Stories to Ignite Performance and Be More Successful.* Kaplan Publishing.

39 Fredrickson, B., et al. (2013). *A Functional Genomic Perspective on Human Well-Being.* Proceedings of the National Academy of Sciences.

40 Seligman, M.E.P. (2002). *Authentic Happiness: Using the New Psychology to Realize Your Potential for Lasting Fulfillment.* Simon & Shuster.

41 Csikszentmihalyi, M. (1990). *Flow: The Psychology of Optimal Experience.* Harper & Row, New York.

42 Fredrickson, B., et al. (2013). *A Functional Genomic Perspective on Human Well-Being.* Proceedings of the National Academy of Sciences.

43 Calfas, J., & Chapman, B. (July 6, 2020). "Gun Violence Marked Fourth of July Weekend in Cities Across the U.S.: Chicago, New York and Atlanta Saw a Surge in Shootings; Young Children Were Among the Fatalities," *The Wall Street Journal*

44 Duckworth, A. (2016). *Grit: The Power of Passion and Perseverance*. Scribner/Simon & Schuster.

45 Duckworth, A.L., et al. (2007). "Grit: Perseverance and Passion for Long-Term Goals." *Journal of Personality and Social Psychology*, 92(6): 1087-1101.

46 Duckworth, A. (2016). *Grit: The Power of Passion and Perseverance*. Scribner/Simon & Schuster.

47 Duckworth, A. (2016). *Grit: The Power of Passion and Perseverance*. Scribner/Simon & Schuster.

48 Duckworth, A.L., Gendler, T., & Gross, J. (2016). "Situational Strategies for Self-Control." *Perspectives on Psychological Science*, 11(1): 35-55.

49 Bowen, S., & Marlatt, A. (2009). "Surfing the Urge: Brief Mindfulness-Based Intervention for College Student Smokers." *Psychol Addict Behav*, 23(4): 666-671. doi:10.1037/a0017127.

50 Park, N., & Peterson, C. (2006). "Moral Competence and Character Strengths Among Adolescents: The Development and Validation of the Values in Action Inventory of Strengths for Youth." *Journal of Adolescence*, 29: 891-909. Park, N., Peterson, C., & Seligman, M.E.P. (2006). "Character strengths in fifty-four nations and the fifty US states." *Journal of Positive Psychology*, 1: 118-129.

51 Duhigg, C. (2012). *The Power of Habit: Why We Do What We Do in Life and Business*. Random House, New York.

52 Damasio, A.R. (2010). *Self Comes to Mind: Constructing the Conscious Brain*. Pantheon Books, New York.

53 Walker, M.P. (2017). *Why We Sleep: Unlocking the Power of Sleep and Dreams*. Scribner, New York.

54 Squire, L.R., Genzel, L., Wixted, J.T., & Morris, R.G. (2015). "Memory consolidation." *Cold Spring Harbor Perspectives in Biology*, 7(8), a021766. https://doi.org/10.1101/cshperspect.a021766.

55 Walker, M.P. (2017). *Why We Sleep: Unlocking the Power of Sleep and Dreams*. Scribner, New York.

56 Walker, M.P. (2017). *Why We Sleep: Unlocking the Power of Sleep and Dreams*. Scribner, New York.

57 Walker, M.P. (2017). *Why We Sleep: Unlocking the Power of Sleep and Dreams*. Scribner, New York.

58 FDNY Ten House, Engine Company 10, and Ladder Company 10, 124 Liberty Street, are across the street from the World Trade Center site. On 9/11 five firefighters from Ten House were killed, and the house itself was

almost destroyed by debris. A makeshift memorial of flowers, pictures, and notes adorned the exterior walls, scaffolding, and fencing near the building.

59 Shortly before 9/11, Leslie Sias had left the US Navy where he served as a chaplain. Moved by the experience of 9/11, he rejoined the Navy and resumed his duties as a chaplain. He is scheduled to retire next year after 28 years of service ranging from Afghanistan to Walter Reed Hospital.

60 DiAngelo, R.J. (2018). *White Fragility: Why It's So Hard for White People to Talk About Racism.* Beacon Press, Boston, MA.

61 Corcoran, R. (2010). *Trustbuilding: An Honest Conversation on Race, Reconcilliation, and Responsibility.* University of Virginia Press, Charlottesville, VA.

62 Corcoran, R. (2010). *Trustbuilding: An Honest Conversation on Race, Reconcilliation, and Responsibility.* Page 14. University of Virginia Press, Charlottesville, VA.

63 Corcoran, R. (2010). *Trustbuilding: An Honest Conversation on Race, Reconcilliation, and Responsibility.* Page 72. University of Virginia Press, Charlottesville, VA.

64 Corcoran, R. (2010). *Trustbuilding: An Honest Conversation On Race, Reconcilliation, And Responsibility.* Page 150. University of Virginia Press, Charlottesville, VA.

65 Crawford, N.C. (2018). "United States Budgetary Costs of the Post-9/11 Wars Through FY2019: $5.9 Trillion Spent and Obligated." Watson Institute of International & Public Affairs, Brown University. Downloaded July 18, 2020, from https://watson.brown.edu/costsofwar/files/cow/imce/papers/2018/ Crawford_Costs%20of%20War%20Estimates%20Through%20 FY2019%20.pdf.

66 Lucas, D. (2019). "Measuring the Cost of Bailouts February." MIT Golub Center for Finance and Policy. Downloaded July 18, 2020, from http://gcfp.mit.edu/wp-content/uploads/2019/02/BailoutsV12.pdf.

67 Noel, N., Pinder, D., Stewart S., & Wright, J. (2019). "The Economic Impact of Closing the Racial Wealth Gap." McKinsey & Company. Downloaded July 18, 2020 from https://www.mckinsey.com/ industries/public-sector/our-insights/the-economic-impact-of-closing-the-racial-wealth-gap#0.

68 Artiga, S., Orgera, K., & Pham, O. (2020), "Disparities in Health and Health Care: Five Key Questions and Answers." Kaiser Family Foundation. Downloaded July 18, 2020, from https://www.kff.org/disparities-policy/issue-brief/disparities-in-health-and-health-care-five-key-questions-and-answers/#:~: text=Moreover%2C%20health%20disparities%20are%20 costly,losses%20due%20to%20premature%20deaths.

69 Wagner, P., & Rabuy, B. (2017). "Following the Money of Mass Incarceration." Prison Policy Initiative. Downloaded on July 19, 2020, from https://www.prisonpolicy.org/reports/money.html.

70 Hilliard, J. (2019). "New Study Shows Police at Highest Risk for Suicide of Any Profession." Addiction Center. Downloaded on July 19, 2020, from https://www.addictioncenter.com/news/2019/09/police-at-highest-risk-fo r-suicide-than-any-profession/.

71 Spence, D.L., Fox, M., Moore, G.C., Estill, S., & Comrie, N.E.A. (2019). "Law Enforcement Mental Health and Wellness Act: Report to Congress." Washington, DC: US Department of Justice. Downloaded on July 19, 2020, from https://cops.usdoj.gov/RIC/Publications/cops-p370-pub.pdf.